Plantation Capitalism - the Ongoing Battle for the Soul of America

Making Capitalism Work for the People.

Ray Mills Antley, Jr. MD

ISBN13:978-0-996-33260-6

Foreword

"In mercantile and manufacturing towns, where the inferior ranks of people are chiefly maintained by the employment of capital, they are in general industrious, sober and thriving; as in many English and most Dutch towns. In those towns which are principally supported by the constant or occasional residence of a court, and which the inferior ranks of people are maintained by the constant of occasional residence of a court, and in which the inferior ranks of people are chiefly maintained by the spending of revenue, they are in general idle, dissolute, and poor as at Rome, Versailles, Compaigne, and Fontainblue."

- Adam Smith, Wealth of Nations
1776

"Republicans are for both the man and the dollar, but in a pinch, choose the man."

-Abraham Lincoln

Capitalism, where the means of production and distribution are privately owned, and production is guided by markets is a powerful force. However, as will be demonstrated, this does not always serve the needs of society. Capitalism is at its heart a positive feedback control mechanism and inherently unstable. To make capitalism work for man rather than man work for capitalism it is necessary to provide a framework to assure accountability for our political economy. This is an argument for accountability in our political economy. This is an argument for the nation state as the unit of accountability.

In this discussion I will use scientific analogies from biology, a field similar to economics where complex systems are organized in a purposeful way. Both biology, businesses, and nations operate in a dynamic Darwinian milieu where decisions have consequences. Illustrations from history will be used, because the lamp of experience, while imperfect, is often the only light we have to the future. Further, the lamp of history shows that several popular misconceptions, are well, wrong.

In the chapter on Archetypes of Capitalism, I will show that there are two main branches of capitalism - 1) free trading capitalism (i.e. English Capitalism), and 2) nationalist capitalism (The American System). Henry Clay makes an eloquent argument for the American System which I quote almost in its entirety because it is a classic. Its main points are as valid today as they were in 1832. Trading capitalism is the capitalism of empire, national capitalism is the capitalism of nation building. If we want to develop the nation, we should return to the capitalism of nation building.

The star, or rather the anti star, of this book is the Plantation Capitalist. To visualize a Plantation capitalist, imagine you are in Barbados in 1650 growing sugar cane. You need to import workers from somewhere. But where? You decide to import African Slaves because you can buy an African slave for life cheaper than you can work an Irish indentured servant for five years. This improves your margin by driving down your wage expense. Plantation capitalism is where the business owner thinks of his workers a commodity to be bought at the cheapest price- an expense to be minimized. This may make some sense for an individual business owner, but to have this mindset penetrate the leadership of the Nation as a whole, and it has, is ruinous, as quick glance at the national debt will show.

Norman Vincent Peale, in his book "The Power of Positive

Thinking", talked of making one's faith work for them. This book is dedicated to helping make sure that capitalism works for the good of society, rather than society being exploited to serve the needs of the capitalists. The central theme that will be developed is that governments have the right and duty to regulate their economic systems to make sure the needs of the population are met. This regulation will take on several forms:

1)The maintenance of a rough balance of trade or a surplus.
2)The promotion of smaller economic entities rather than large economic entities for several reasons:
   a. To encourage competition.
   b. To retard corruption.
   c. To prevent gross abuse.
   d. To keep the corporate interest aligned with the society from which it came.
   e. To promote accountability of corporations.
   f. To eliminate the concept of "to big to fail".
   g. To facilitate tax collection which becomes problematic for transnational corporations.
3. The collection of Taxes.
4. The maintenance of the technological and industrial might to provide for the common defense. Maintenance of a Department of War. Enforcement of boundaries.
5. The promotion of the general welfare.
6. The administration of justice.
7. The protection of the environment.
8. The education of the young.
9. The facilitation of health both on the job and off.
10. The development of modern infrastructure for transportation, communication, power delivery, waste disposal.

Table of Contents:

Disasters of Capitalism: Plantation Capitalism at Work

"When you take your eyes off Jesus, you begin to sink."
-Reverend Flem McIntosh

There is a social myth that capitalism is a benign force, and left alone will produce a harmonious society growing in wealth. The historic record has many examples of capitalism causing great growth, but there are other darker examples of the unrestrained search for profit causing great misery. The discussion includes Barbados, because the effects of slavery are no abstraction to people of the New World, and the concept of a Plantation Capitalist endeavoring to break the spirit of his workers and reap the reward of not paying them a decent wage is with us still and central to the overall thrust of this book. The Highland clearances are chosen because it shows the clear disloyalty of the Chiefs to their workers, when their workers were their kin, the reason they had title to vast estates, and in times of stress their comrades in arms - none of these bonds of consanguinity, generational comradeship on the field of battle, or sense of gratitude toward the people who had elevated the Duchess of Sutherland to great wealth made any difference to the owners once they saw themselves as capitalists - the love of money conquered all. The Irish potato famine is included because the sheer unnecessary devastation is spectacular, and the inadequate response to the crisis was a result of the incorporation of free trade theory blunting what should have been a Christian call to action. This list is of course, the tip of the iceberg, and similar behavior can be seen in Latin America, the Belgian Congo, India, the Opium War in China.

The founding document of New England, the Mayflower compact, states that the adventure of settlement in a New World was undertaken for the glory of God and the advancements of the Christian faith.

In the name of God, Amen. We, whose names are underwritten, the loyal subjects of our dread Sovereign Lord King James, by the Grace of God, of Great Britain, France, and Ireland, King, defender of the Faith, etc.
Having undertaken, for the Glory of God, and advancements of the Christian faith and honor of our King and Country, a voyage to plant the first colony in the Northern parts of Virginia, do by these presents, solemnly and mutually, in the presence of God, and one another, covenant and combine ourselves together into a civil body politic; for our better ordering, and preservation and furtherance of the ends aforesaid; and by virtue hereof to enact, constitute, and frame, such just and equal laws, ordinances, acts, constitutions, and offices, from time to time, as shall be thought most meet and convenient for the general good of the colony; unto which we promise all due submission and obedience.
In witness whereof we have hereunto subscribed our names at Cape Cod the 11th of November, in the year of the reign of our Sovereign Lord King James, of England, France, and Ireland, the eighteenth, and of Scotland the fifty-fourth, 1620.

The Serpent in the Garden: Plantation Capitalism Rears its Ugly Head

Alternatively, the founding of Barbados in 1627 was undertaken in a relentless search for profit. During the first 15 years of colonization, pioneering in Barbados was hard work. Once the land was cleared, crops for food were planted. Then cash crops with low margins- tobacco and cotton were planted. Initially labor consisted mostly of indentured servants. This labor was fairly cheap with many of the young men kidnapped in England and transported to Barbados. However, because of the thin margins of tobacco and cotton, the profits were not great.

In the 1640's sugar cane was introduced. This was a high margin crop and transformed the colony. The price of land went up. Smaller planters were pushed out and tenant farmers displaced off their lands. "Virginia might be the Old Dominion and Massachusetts the Bible commonwealth, but Barbados was something much more tangible: the richest colony in English America."[1]

The capitalist culture that formed was "individualistic, competitive, and highly materialistic."

Since profits were up, one might expect the laborers to experience an improving quality of life. However, the Plantation Capitalists saw they could make more money by lowering their cost of labor.

Initially the labor on the island was young white males. The Barbadian capitalists were turning a profit using indentured servants. However, it was cheaper to buy an African slave for life than to hire an indentured servant for five years. In addition, white workers were more expensive to feed, clothe, and house. The capitalists therefore adopted the Spanish/ Brazilian model of African slavery so they could maximize their profits. In 1638 there were 200 African slaves out of a population of 6000, in 1643 there were 6,400 African slaves out of a population of 25,000, and in 1650 the European population was 30,000 and the African population 12,800. By 1660 the population of Barbados was over half slave (26,000 white and 27,000 black).

The treatment of both labor groups was brutal. The sugar

production increased as Cromwell completed the conquest of Ireland. Thousands of Irish were sent to Barbados. Others were sent by corrupt judges. "Barbadozz'd " was a verb meaning to be Shanghaied to the colonies. Marcellus Rivers (an Englishman of Royalist sympathies) and seventy of his friends were on the receiving end of this. He was arrested during the Salisbury Rising (suppressed by Cromwell) , imprisoned for a year, and shipped to Barbados in 1656. He was sold for 1550 lbs of sugar. He testified in Parliament that he was "whipt at the whipping posts, as Rogues, for their mafters pleafure," he slept in sites worse "than hogs in England", ate nothing but potatoes and drank nothing but water.

Initially indentured servants were given 5 - 10 acres of land upon surviving 5 years of service, but after 1635 the supply of land was constrained so this practice ceased. The level of violence rose with more frequent and brutal punishment with the servants referred to as "white slaves". The servants revolted and were suppressed. The whippings and language were outside of behavioral norms in England (although there was plenty of precedent for such cruelty in Ireland). "Truly I have seen such cruelty there done to Servants. as I did not think one Christian could have done to another," said Richard Ligon of Barbodos. When the labor force was switched to slavery, the opportunities for free white labour diminished and up to 12,000 of the settlers left.[3]

The treatment of the African slaves was even worse. The slaves died rapidly and were replaced with new imports rather than improved conditions. 130,000 slaves were brought to Barbados between 1640 and 1700 but only 50,000 were still alive at the turn of the new century. The slaves were housed in huts made of cane stalks and palm leaves. The slaves worked six days a week 10-11 hours per day. English law had no precedent for chattel slavery so the Plantation Capitalists invented one. In the Barbados Slave Act of 1661 an white indentured servant striking his master incurred an was additional year of servitude. For the first offense an African slave severely "whipt", on the second the slave would have his or her nose split and face branded, and on the third offense he would face "greater corporal punishment" - probably death. This level of physical disfigurement was new to English law. The slave code stated that blacks were "an heathenish, brutish, and an uncertaine, dangerous, kind of people." The master could punish and work his slaves as he saw fit. There was no protection from whipping, castration, or death. The master did have to provide minimal clothing. Barbadians punished defiant slaves by"putting a man to dry"- hanging a man in an iron cage until he died of hunger and thirst as a method of intimidation. In 1694, for stealing a pig, judges ordered a man quartered. This cruelty was justified on racial grounds and on the grounds that they were not Christians. When the Quakers tried to make them Christians, the Barbados government fined them 7000 pounds, executed one of the Quakers, and nailed their meeting house shut.[4]

The importation of slaves from Africa brought malaria, yellow fever, hookworm, yaws, guinea worm, leprosy, and elephantiasis. This brought the stench of death to the island. In 1647 Richard Ligon noted that almost all the Barbadians were,"new men, for few or none of them that first set foot there, were now living." Parish registries of the white population in the 1650's recorded four times as many deaths as marriages and three times as many deaths as births. The love of money had converted what should have been a tropical paradise to raise families into a vision of Hell worthy of a Hieronymous Bosch painting that lasted from 1640 - 1833 when the English emancipated the slaves of the British Empire.[5] Between 1620 and 1700 New England had 21,000 immigrants but the population grew to 91,000.[6] Barbados imported 130,000 slaves of which only 50,000 were alive in 1700.[7] The white population of freemen collapsed to 15,000. The place made money for a few but at a huge human cost. If man is the measure of all things, Barbados was a miserable failure. If you focus on God, your thoughts will tend to encompass the entire community of your fellow man. If you focus on money, you focus on money.

This is Plantation Capitalism in its raw form. Plantation Capitalism is a variant of Anglo Saxon free market Capitalism. This is a motif that will be explored in this book.

It has several elements:

1) It is a for profit operation. It is not about community development.
2) Labor is sourced from wherever it is cheapest, like copper or iron. In Barbados, labor was completely commoditized.
3) Labor is not valued highly since it is cheap and there is a psychological chasm between labor and ownership and management.
4) In its worst form, Extractive Plantation Capitalism, there is absentee ownership who value the operation solely for the cash flow.
5) Labor is not developed. Training of labor is limited.
6) The market is not the workers. The less the workers consume, the better.
7) Often the the workers and the owners do not pray together. (The Irish Catholics and the English Protestants, the African Methodist Episcopal Church and the Methodists, etc.)
8) There is often a racial ethnic nature of the Plantation Capitalism. In the Ulster Plantation, Calvinist Protestants were brought in to keep the native Catholic Irish in check. In Barbados, African slaves were brought in but a cadre of "poor whites" were retained to preserve the large landowners power to intimidate the slaves. Neither the poor whites or the slaves were respected of course.

Initially Plantation Capitalists used racism as an excuse to treat their African workers brutally and created distance between the free workers and the slaves so the common interests of workers could be suppressed. Today, Plantation Capitalists, in a form of jujitsu, use the language of diversity to obscure the fact they are bringing in cheap labor to destroy the wage scale and increase their margins.

9) It runs on fear and greed. There is often a militarized violent undertone.

Plantation Capitalism needs several things to thrive.

1) It needs a market- an external market. Since the workers are oppressed and underpaid, it needs an external market. It is not a complete system since it needs an external market. In Barbados the market was Europe.

2) It needs access to cheap workers. In Barbados the labor was so cheap that people died faster than they reproduced which is evidence they were treated horribly.

3) It needs psychological distance between the workers and the owners. Given time, the workers and the owners will form a better more egalitarian society if this psychological distance is breached. The relationships between house slaves and field hands and their masters were quite different.

Note that free Capitalists making laws on slavery based on property rights were far more inhuman than the feudal aristocracy of Europe. You will not find people being dried out and castrated in the legends of King Arthur or in the stories of Robin Hood. Authority that depended on the divine right of kings in a Christian country had some recognition that even the serfs were children of the heavenly Father. There were precedents for such inhuman behavior, of course, in the pre Christian writings of Greece, Rome, and Egypt. Islam also had developed history of slavery. But slavery was new to English Law and was developed to oppress labor and make greater profits.

This experiment of allowing capitalists to make the laws allowed many of the absentee owners to live very well in England. Barbados colonized South Carolina and brought the Barbadian slave code to North America(1696). Plantation life spread from this point across the Deep South. The principal of driving down the price of labor to increase the profit margin is of course the invisible hand of capitalism at work. It is not necessarily a forward thinking hand. South Carolina, the direct descendant of Barbados, was the home of John C. Calhoun and the secessionist movement. In 1860 it seceded, in 1861 it fired the first shot and started the Civil War; by the war's end between 30 -35% of the military age population was dead, and Sherman had left the state a bankrupt smoking ruin.

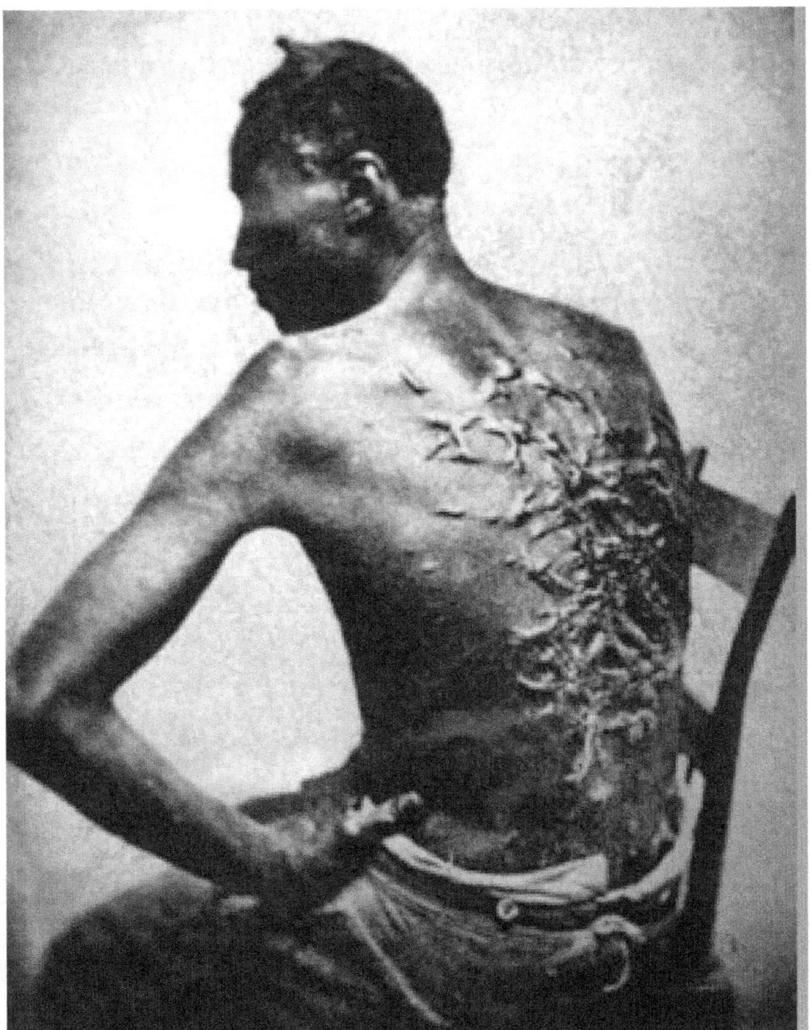

Adam Smith was aware that capitalists freed of the constraints of the government had a tendency to abuse their workers. A general dislike of slavery and oppression can be seen as a subtext in several of his passages. (page 553-554 The Wealth of Nations-Prosperity of New Colonies).

In all European colonies the culture of sugar - cane is carried on by negro slaves… …and in the good management of their slaves the French planters, I think it is generally allowed are superior to the English. The law, so far as it gives some weak protection to the slave against the violence of his master, is likely to be better executed in a colony where the government is in a great measure arbitrary, than in one where it is altogether free. In every country where the unfortunate law of slavery is established, the magistrate, when he protects the slave, intermeddles in some measure in the management of the private property of the master; and in a free country, where the master is perhaps either a member of the colony assembly, or an elector of such a member, he dare not do this except with the greatest caution and circumspection. The respect which he is obliged to pay to the master, renders it more difficult for him to protect the slave. But in a country where the government is in a great measure arbitrary, where it is usual for the magistrate to intermeddle even in the management of the private property of individuals, and to send them, perhaps, a letter de cachet if they do not manage it according to his liking , it is much easier for him to give some protection to the slave; and common humanity naturally predisposes him to do so. The protection of the magistrate renders the slave less contemptible in the eyes of his master, who is thereby induced to consider him with more regard, and to treat him with more gentleness. Gentle usage renders the slave not only more faithful, but more intelligent, and therefore, upon double account, more useful. He approaches more to the condition of a free servant, and may possess some degree of integrity and attachment to his master's interest, virtues which frequently belong to free servants, but which can never belong to a slave, who is treated as slaves commonly are in countries where the master is perfectly free and secure.

That the condition of a slave is better in an arbitrary than under a free government is, I believe, supported by the history of all ages and nations. In the Roman history, the first time we read of the magistrate interposing to protect the slave from the violence of his master is under the emperors. When Vedius Pollio, in the presence of Augustus, ordered one of his slaves, who had committed a slight fault, to be cut into pieces and thrown into his fish-pond in order to feed his fishes, the emperor commanded him, with indignation, to emancipate immediately, not only that slave, but all the others that belonged to him. Under the republic no magistrate could have had authority enough to protect the slave, much less punish the master.

It is tempting to think that abuse of workers stopped with the Civil War. Capital, however, values workers only according to their scarcity. Father Luis, a young Spanish priest, went to Guatemala in the 1960's. He went to minister to the Indians in the mountains. Large numbers of his flock went down to work in the lowland plantations. He followed the workers to see how they were doing. He found them living in deplorable conditions, under a roof with no walls, sick with tropical diseases. They had difficulty buying the medicines to treat their diseases and were dying in great numbers. As he looked at the plantation, he saw a fine building with air conditioning.

"Does the owner live there?", he asked.

"No.", came the reply.

"Does the overseer live there?", he asked.

"No." ,came the reply.

"Well who does live there?", he asked.

"The horses.", came the reply.

"The horses?", he asked. "How do the horses have a fine building with air conditioning and the farm workers have no protection from mosquitos?"

"When a horse dies it costs money to import another from the United States."

"And the workers?", he asked.
"When the Indians die, more come down from the mountains." , came the reply.[2]

The North American Free Trade Agreement can be thought of as law written by capitalists to allow more workers come down from the mountain to drive down wages. The central valley of California, some of the richest land on the planet, would be the poorest state in the union if it was a separate state. This is the plantation system, no longer able to import completely disenfranchised workers, slaves, from Africa, now importing disenfranchised workers from Latin America. Slaves can be thought of as workers with no political rights. Illegal immigrants have the ability to sell their labor to the highest bidder but lack political and legal rights to enforce contracts and vote for better conditions are somewhere between free labor and slaves. Mr Gingrich and others have proposed giving undocumented workers a right to work but not to vote. Proposals like that of Mr. Gingrich to formalize a servant class should be vehemently resisted as an assault on free labor. Capitalists are using globalization to arbitrage wages to the lowest possible level. Essentially they aim to set global wages where labor is under the greatest duress- typically where people are in the greatest pain. This could value humans below horses- it has happened before. Actually, the plan to drive down wages is working. Median US wages have been going down since 1973.

1. Walter Edgar, *South Carolina,A History*(University of South Carolina Press,1998) p37.
2. Father Luis told this story in the fall of 1983 in Charlotte, NC. I believe the story to be true but have no independent confirmation.
3. Alan Taylor, American Colonies,*The Settling of North America*, (Penguin Books,2001), p 208.
4. Ibid., p 212-214.
5. Ibid., p 217.
6. Ibid., p 170.
7. Ibid., p 212.

Another example of Capitalism not serving the general needs of the population is the Highland Clearances. Karl Marx wrote an article in 1853 on the Duchess of Sutherland.

Articles by Karl Marx in *The People's Paper*
The Duchess of Sutherland and Slavery

Published in: *The People's Paper*, No. 45, March 12 1853;

> **London, Friday, January 21, 1853** — During the present momentary slackness in political affairs, the address of the Stafford House Assembly of Ladies to their sisters in America upon the subject of Negro-Slavery, and the "affectionate and Christian address of many thousands of the women of the United States of America to their sisters, the women of England", upon white slavery, have proved a god-send to the press. Not one of the British papers was ever struck by the circumstance that the Stafford House Assembly took place at the palace under the Presidency of the Duchess of Sutherland, and yet the names of Stafford and Sutherland should have been sufficient to class the philanthropy of the British Aristocracy — a philanthropy which chooses its objects as far distant from home as possible, and rather on that than on this side of the ocean.
>
> The history of the wealth of the Sutherland family is the history of the ruin and of the expropriation of the Scotch-Gaelic population from its native soil. As far back as the 10th century, the Danes had landed in Scotland, conquered the plains of Caithness, and driven back the aborigines into the mountains. Mhoir-Fhear-Chattaibh, as he was called in Gaelic, or the "Great Man of Sutherland", had always found his companions-in-arms ready to defend him at risk of their lives against all his enemies, Danes or Scots, foreigners or natives. After the revolution which drove the Stuarts from

Britain, private feuds among the petty chieftains of Scotland became less and less frequent, and the British Kings, in order to keep up at least a semblance of dominion in these remote districts, encouraged the levying of family regiments among the chieftains, a system by which these *lairds* were enabled to combine modern military establishments with the ancient *clan* system in such a manner as to support one by the other.

Now, in order to distinctly appreciate the usurpation subsequently carried out, we must first properly understand what the clan meant. The clan belonged to a form of social existence which, in the scale of historical development, stands a full degree below the feudal state; viz., the *patriarchal* state of society. "Klaen", in Gaelic, means children. Every one of the usages and traditions of the Scottish Gaels reposes upon the supposition that the members of the clan belong to one and the same family. The "great man", the chieftain of the clan, is on the one hand quite as arbitrary, on the other quite as confined in his power, by consanguinity, &c., as every father of a family. To the clan, to the family, belonged the district where it had established itself, exactly as in Russia, the land occupied by a community of peasants belongs, not to the individual peasants, but to the community. Thus the district was the common property of the family. There could be no more question, under this system, of private property, in the modern sense of the word, than there could be of comparing the social existence of the members of the clan to that of individuals living in the midst of our modern society. The division and subdivision of the land corresponded to the military functions of the single members of the clan. According to their military abilities, the chieftain entrusted to them the several allotments, cancelled or enlarged according to his pleasure the tenures of the individual officers, and these officers again distributed to their vassals and under-vassals every separate plot of land. But the district at large always remained the property of the clan, and, however the claims of individuals might vary, the tenure remained the same; nor were the contributions for the common defense, or the tribute for the Laird, who at once was leader in battle and chief magistrate in peace, ever increased. Upon the whole, every plot of land was cultivated by the same family, from generation to generation, under fixed imposts. These imposts were insignificant, more a tribute by which the supremacy of the "great man" and of his officers was acknowledged, than a rent of land in a modern sense, or a source of revenue. The officers directly subordinate to the "great man" were called "Taksmen", and the district entrusted to their care, "Tak". Under then were placed inferior officers, at the head of every hamlet, and under these stood the peasantry.

Thus you see, the clan is nothing but a family organized in a military manner, quite as little defined by laws, just as closely hemmed in by traditions, as any family. But the land is the *property of the family*, in the midst of which differences of rank, in spite of consanguinity, do prevail as well as in all the ancient Asiatic family communities.

The first usurpation took place, after the expulsion of the Stuarts, by the establishment of the family Regiments. From that moment, *pay* became the principal source of revenue of the Great Man, the Mhoir-Fhear-Chattaibh. Entangled in the dissipation of the Court of London, he tried to squeeze as much money as possible out of his officers, and they applied the same system of their inferiors. The ancient tribute was transformed into fixed money contracts. In one respect these contracts constituted a progress, by fixing the traditional imposts; in another respect they were a usurpation, inasmuch as the "great man" now took the position of landlord toward the "taksmen" who again took toward the peasantry that of farmers. And as the "great men" now required money no less than the "taksmen", a production not only for direct consumption but for export and exchange also became necessary; the system of national production had to be changed, the hands superseded by this change had to be got rid of. Population, therefore, decreased. But that it as yet was kept up in a certain manner, and that man, in the 18th century, was not yet openly sacrificed to net-revenue, we see from a passage in Steuart, a Scotch political economist, whose work was published 10 years before Adam Smith's, where it says (Vol.1, Chap.16):

"The rent of these lands is very trifling compared to their extent, but compared to the number of mouths which a farm maintains, it will perhaps be found that a plot of land in the highlands of Scotland feeds ten times more people than a farm of the same extent in the richest provinces."

That even in the beginnings of the 19th century the rental imposts were very small, is shown by the work of Mr Loch (1820), the steward of the Countess of Sutherland, who directed the improvements on her estates. He gives for instance the rental of the Kintradawell estate for 1811, from which it appears that up to then, every family was obliged to pay a yearly impost of a few shillings in money, a few fowls, and some days' work, at the highest.

It was only after 1811 that the ultimate and real usurpation was enacted, the forcible transformation of *clan-property* into the *private property*, in the modern sense, *of the Chief*. The person who stood at the head of this economical revolution was a female Mehemet Ali, who had well digested her Malthus — the Countess of Sutherland, alias Marchioness of Stafford.

Let us first state that the ancestors of the Marchioness of Stafford were the "great men" of the most northern part of

Scotland, of very near three-quarters of Sutherlandshire. This country is more extensive than many French Departments or small German Principalities. when the Countess of Sutherland inherited these estates, which she afterward brought to her husband, the Marquis of Stafford, afterward Duke of Sutherland, the population of them was already reduced to 15,000. My lady Countess resolved upon a radical economical reform, and determined upon transforming the whole tract of country into sheep-walks. From 1814 to 1820, these 15,000 inhabitants, about 3,000 families, were systematically expelled and exterminated. All their villages were demolished and burned down, and all their fields converted into pasturage. British soldiers were commanded for this execution, and came to blows with the natives. An old woman refusing to quit her hut was burned in the flames of it. Thus my lady Countess appropriated to herself 794,000 acres of land, which from time immemorial had belonged to the clan. In the exuberance of her generosity she allotted to the expelled natives about 6,000 acres — two acres per family. These 6,000 acres had been lying waste until then, and brought no revenue to the proprietors. The Countess was generous enough to sell the acre at 2s 6d on an average, to the clan-men who for centuries past had shed their blood for her family. The whole of the unrightfully appropriated clan-land she divided into 29 large sheep farms, each of them inhabited by one single family, mostly English farm-laborers; and in 1821 the 15,000 Gaels had already been superseded by 131,000 sheep.

A portion of the aborigines had been thrown upon the sea-shore, and attempted to live by fishing. They became amphibious, and, as an English author says, lived half on land and half on water, and after all did not live upon both.

Sismondi, in his *Etudes Sociales*, observes with regard to this expropriation of the Gaels from Sutherlandshire — an example, which, by-the-by, was imitated by other "great men" of Scotland:

> "The large extent of seignorial domains is not a circumstance peculiar to Britain. In the whole Empire of Charlemagne, in the whole Occident, entire provinces were usurped by the warlike chiefs, who had them cultivated for their own account by the vanquished, and sometimes by their own companions-in-arms. During the 9th and 10th centuries the Counties of Maine, Anjou, Poitou were for the Counts of these provinces rather three large estates than principalities. Switzerland, which in so many respects resembles Scotland, was at that time divided among a small number of Seigneurs. If the Counts of Kyburg, of Lenzburg, of Habsburg, of Gruyeres had been protected by British laws, they would have been in the same position as the Earls of Sutherland; some of them would perhaps have had the same taste for improvement as the Marchioness of Stafford, and more than one republic might have disappeared from the Alps in order to make room for flocks of sheep. Not the most despotic monarch in Germany would be allowed to attempt anything of the sort."

Mr Loch, in his defense of the Countess of Sutherland (1820), replies to the above as follows:

"Why should there be made an exception to the rule adopted in every other case, just for this particular case? Why should the absolute authority of the landlord over his land be sacrificed to the public interest and to motives which concern the public only?"

And why, then, should the slave-holders in the Southern States of North America sacrifice their private interest to the philanthropic grimaces of her Grace, the Duchess of Sutherland?

The British aristocracy, who have everywhere superseded man by bullocks and sheep, will, in a future not very distant, be superseded, in turn, by these useful animals.

The process of *clearing estates*, which, in Scotland, we have just now described, was carried out in England in the 16th, 17th, and 18th centuries. Thomas Morus already complains of it in the beginning of the 16th century. It was performed in Scotland in the beginning of the 19th, and in Ireland it is now in full progress. The noble Viscount Palmerston, too, some years ago cleared of men his property in Ireland, exactly in the manner described above.

If of any property it ever was true that it was *robbery*, it is literally true of the property of the British aristocracy. Robbery of Church property, robbery of commons, fraudulent transformation, accompanied by murder, of feudal and patriarchal property into private property — these are the titles of British aristocrats to their possessions. And what services in this latter process were performed by a servile class of lawyers, you may see from an English lawyer of the last century, Dalrymple, who, in his *History of Feudal Property*, very naively proves that every law or deed concerning property was interpreted by the lawyers, in England, when the middle class rose in wealth in favor of the *middle class* — in Scotland, where the nobility enriched themselves, in favor of the *nobility* — in either case it was interpreted in a sense hostile to the *people*.

The above Turkish reform by the Countess of Sutherland was justifiable, at least, from a Malthusian point of view. Other Scottish noblemen went further. Having superseded human beings by sheep, they superseded sheep by game, and the pasture grounds by forests. At the head of these was the Duke of Atholl.

"After the conquest, the Norman Kings afforested large portions of the soil of England, in much the same way as the landlords here are now doing with the Highlands.

(R. Somers, Letters on the Highlands, 1848)

As for a large number of the human beings expelled to make room for the game of the Duke of Atholl, and the sheep of the Countess of Sutherland, where did they fly to, where did they find a home?

In the United States of America.

The enemy of British Wage-Slavery has a right to condemn Negro-Slavery; a Duchess of Sutherland, a Duke of Atholl, a Manchester Cotton-lord — never!

In the above editorial, Marx explains how a feudal system was changed into a capitalist system with the chief being given title to the whole land and how behaving as a pure capitalist abused the people who as a chief he should have been taking care of. This is an example of capitalism not being made to serve the needs of the many but to serve the needs of the one with the invisible hand causing devastation of a culture and families.

In 1807 Elizabeth Gordon, 19th Countess of Sutherland, inspected her inheritance with her husband Lord Stafford wrote, "he is seized as much as I and with the rage of improvements, and we both turn our attention with the greatest of energy to turnips". They also began turning the land over to sheep farming which produced a greater cash flow for the owner. That year her overseers began to evict her tenants to make way for sheep. 90 families were forced to leave their crops in the ground and move their cattle to land they were offered on the coast.

The Sutherland's overseer William Young hired Patrick Sellar as his agent . Sellar personally evicted longtime tenants and burned down their houses to make sure they never returned. Many starved and froze to death where their homes had once been. On seeing the starving tenants on her husbands estate, the Duchess of Sutherland wrote a friend in England, "Scotch people are of a happier constitution and do not fatten like the larger breed of animals."

Donald McLeod bore witness to these evictions:

"The houses had been all built...by the tenants and their ancestors and were their property by right if not by law. They were timbered chiefly with bog fir which makes excellent roofing but is very inflammable....

In former removals the tenants had been allowed to carry away this timber to erect houses in their new allotments, but now a more summary mode was adopted, by setting fire to the houses. The able bodied men were away with their cattle or otherwise engaged at a distance, so that the immediate sufferers by the general house burning that now commenced were the aged and infirm, the women and children.....

These proceedings were carried on with the greatest rapidity and with the most reckless cruelty. The cries of the victims, the confusion, the despair and horror painted on the countenances of one party,and the exulting ferocity of the other, beggar all description....

John Mckay's wife, Ravigill, in attempting to pull down her house in the absence of her husband, to preserve the timber, fell through the roof. She was in consequence, taken with premature labor, and in that state was exposed to the open air and the view of bystanders. Donald Monro, Garvott, lying in fever, was turned out of his house and exposed to the elements. Donald McBeath, an infirm bed ridden old man , had the house unroofed over him, and was , in that state, exposed to the wind and rain until death put a period to his sufferings. I was present at the pulling down and burning of the house of William Chisholm, Badinloskin, in which was lying his wife's mother, an old bed ridden woman of near 100 years of age, none of the family being present. I informed the persons about to set fire to the house of this circumstance, and prevailed on them to wait til Mr Sellar came. On his arrival I told him of the poor old woman being in a condition unfit for removal. He replied, "Damn her, the old witch, she has lived too long; let her burn." Fire was immediately set to the house, and the blankets in which she was carried were in flames before she could be got out. She was placed in a little shed, and it was with great difficulty they were prevented from firing it also. The old woman's daughter arrived while the house was on fire, and assisted the neighbors in removing her mother from the flames and smoke, presenting a picture of horror I shall never forget, but cannot attempt to describe. She died within 5 days."[8]

In April 1815 Sellar was arrested and charged with "willfull fire raising...most aggravated circumstances of cruelty, if not murder." A jury of rich landowners and merchants acquitted Sellar. In 1816 Sellar continued to clear Sutherlandshire of people to make way for sheep. In 1818 he retired to an estate given him by Lord and Lady Stafford.

Kenneth McKay became the chief local authority and continued the evictions.

Donald McLeod describes another clearing of part of the parishes of Farr, Rogart, Golspie, and the whole parish of Kildonan in May 1819:

"The consternation and confusion were extreme. Little or no time was given for the removal of persons or property; the people striving to remove the sick and helpless before the fire should reach them; next, struggling to save the most valuable of their effects. The cries of the women and children, the roaring of the affrighted cattle, hunted at the same time by the yelling dogs of the shepherds amid the smoke and fire, altogether presented a scene that completely baffles description- it required to be seen to be believed.

A dense cloud of smoke enveloped the whole country by day, and even extended out to sea. At night an awfully grand but terrific scene presented itself- all the houses in an extensive district in flames at once. I myself ascended a height about eleven o'clock in the evening, and counted two hundred and fifty blazing houses, many of the owners of which I personally knew, but whose condition - whether in or out of the flames- I could not tell. The conflagration lasted six days, till the whole of the buildings were reduced to ashes or smoking ruins. During one of these days a boat actually lost her way in the dense smoke as she approached the shore, but at night was enabled to reach a landing place by the lurid light of the flames."[9]

In October, 1830 when Donald McLeod was working in Wick:

"..a party of eight men...entered my dwelling (at) about 3 o'clock, just as the family were rising from dinner.

The party allowed no time for parley, but having put out the family with violence, proceeded to fling out the furniture, bedding and other effects in quick time, and after extinguishing the fire, proceeded to nail up the doors and windows in the face of the helpless woman.... Messengers had (previously) been dispatched--warning all the surrounding inhabitants, at the peril of similar treatment, against affording shelter, or assistance, to wife, child, or animal belonging to Donald Macleod. ...After spending most part of the night in fruitless attempts to obtain the shelter of a roof or hovel, my wife at last returned to collect some of her scattered furniture, and (built) with her own hands a temporary shelter against the walls of her late comfortable residence...(but) the wind dispersed (the) materials as fast as she could collect them.

Buckling up her children...in the best manner she could, she left them in charge of the eldest (who was only seven years old), giving them such victuals as she could collect, and prepared to take the road for Caithness (in search of her husband). She had not proceeded many miles when she met with a good Samaritan and acquaintance...Donald Macdonald, who, disregarding the danger incurred, opened his door to her, refreshed and consoled her, and still under cover of night, accompanied her to the dwelling of (a friend), William Innes...of Sandside."[10]

Donald McLeod relates a story from the time of the Crimean War when after many years of exploitation and destruction the Duke of Sutherland returned to Dunrobin Castle in Sutherland shire to recruit men for the 93rd Highland regiment. (This was not from direct observation as is much of his work but related to him by a friend):

"....the Duke himself left London for Sutherland, he arrived at Dunrobin about 10 days ago, and after presenting himself upon the streets of Golspie and Brora, he called a meeting of the male inhabitants of the parishes of Clyne, Rogart, and Golspie; the meeting was well attended, upwards of 400 were punctual at the hour, his Grace in his carriage with his military staff and factors appeared shortly after, the people gave him a hearty cheer; his Grace took the chair. Three or four clerks took their seats at the table, and loosened down bulky packages of bank notes, and spread out platefuls of glittering gold. The Duke addressed the people very serious, and entered upon the necessity of going to war with Russia, and the danger of allowing the Czar to have more power than what he holds already, of his cruel despotic reign in Russia, &c, likewise praising the Queen and her government, rulers and nobles of Great Britain, who stood so much in need of men to put and keep down the Tyrant Russia, and foil him in his wicked schemes to take possession of Turkey. In concluding his address, which was often cheered, he told the able bodied men that his clerks were ready to take down the names of all who were willing to enlist in the 93rd Highlanders that the clerk would give him, there and then, 6 pounds sterling, those who would rather any other corps would get 3 pounds, all from his own private purse, independent of the government bounty; after many silly flattering decrements, he sat down to see the result, but there was no movement among the people; after sitting for a long time looking at the clerks, and them at him, at last his anxious looks at the people assumed a somewhat indignant appearance, when he suddenly rose up and asked what was the cause of the non attention to the proposal that he made, but no reply; it was the silence of the grave-- still standing, his Grace suddenly asked the cause; but to no reply; at last an old man leaning upon his staff was observed moving towards the Duke, and when he approached near enough, he answered his grace something like as follows: "I am sorry for the response your Grace's proposals are meeting here today, so near the spot where your maternal mother, by giving forty eight hours notice, marshaled fifteen hundred men, to pick out of them the nine hundred she required, but there is a cause for it, a grievous cause, and as your Grace demands to know it I must tell you, as I see none else are inclined in this assembly to do it. Your Grace's mother and predecessors applied to our fathers for men upon former occasions, and our fathers responded to their call, they made liberal promises which neither them nor you performed; we are, we think, a little wiser than our fathers, and we estimate your promises of today at the value of theirs, besides you should bear in mind that your predecessors and yourself expelled us in a most cruel and unjust manner from the land which our fathers held in lien from your family for their sons, brothers, cousins, and relations, which was handed over to your parents to keep up their dignity, and to kill the Americans, Turks, French, and the Irish; and these lands are now devoted to rear dumb brute animals, which you and your parents consider of far more value than men. I do assure your Grace that it is the prevailing opinion in this country, that should the Czar of Russia take possession of Dunrobin Castle and of Stafford House next term, that we could not expect worse treatment at his hands than we have experienced at the hands of your family for the last 50 years. Your parents, yourself, and your commissioners, have desolated the glens and straths of Sutherland, where you should find hundreds, yea, thousands of men to meet you and to respond cheerfully to your call, had your parents and yourself kept faith with them. How could your Grace expect to find men where they are not, and the few of them which are to be found among the rubbish and ruins of the country, have more sense than to be decoyed by chaff to the field of slaughter; but one comfort you have, though you cannot find men to fight, you can supply those who will fight with plenty of mutton, beef, and venison." The Duke rose up, put on his hat, and left the field."[11]

-Donald McLeod's, Gloomy Memories in the Highlands of Scotland: Versus Mrs. Harriet Beecher Stowe's Sunny Memories in (England) a Foreign Land, or, a Faithful Picture of the Extirpation of the Celtic Race from the Highlands of Scotland

The Highland clearances are an example of capitalism not serving the needs of the population because the incentives were misallocated. The title to the land and the power of the state was assigned to the aristocracy who decided to run their properties for profit rather than taking care of their people. It is shocking and instructive that the aristocracy had no sense of loyalty to their charges, for in a sense the preservation of their estate in savage earlier centuries had depended on the loyalty of these same subjects to their lords. Even without this shared history, one would hope that a common sense of humanity would have softened the application of for profit capitalism.

The corporation, however, has profitability as its reason for being. It may be difficult for a CEO to justify kindness on his balance sheet, so putting constraints on the activity of the corporation is likely to be necessary to insure that the effects of corporate activities on the people, environment, and society are taken into account.

Dunrobin Castle

The Irish potato famine was a first cousin to the Highland clearances and there are many parallels. The political power was concentrated in an Anglo Irish elite which had an antagonistic historical relationship with their Catholic farm workers. The Parliament which would make the political decisions to address the Potato Famine was in London far away from the the hunger pang. Therefore the response lacked the urgency that would have ensued if people were enduring mass starvation on the Thames. The decision makers in London had absorbed Laissez Faire economic indoctrination which made them insensitive to the humanitarian disaster and made the response far less effective than it might have been. This lack of treating the Irish as fellow citizens during their hour of need was not forgotten but strongly contributed to Irish Nationalism and the dissolution of the Irish portion of the United Kingdom.

Large estates in Ireland were owned by an Anglo Irish aristocracy which often lived in England like Lord Palmerston. 20-30% of the land were owned by absentee landlords. There was if anything, less of a natural affinity of the owners of the plantations and the farm laborers. The native population of Irish was reduced to farming small plots of land which the incredible food value of the potato made a survivable proposition. A single acre could yield six tons of potatoes, enough to feed a family of six for a year without malnutrition. (This is uncannily similar to Marcellus Rivers tale of woe in Barbados where he was fed nothing but potatoes so all the rest of the available land could be devoted to the Barbadian cash crop - sugar). This allowed the rest of the estate to be used for more profitable products such as cattle, butter, peas, beans,etc. .

"The Celtic grazing lands of... Ireland had been used to pasture cows for centuries. The British colonized... the Irish, transforming much of their countryside into an extended grazing land to raise cattle for a hungry consumer market at home... The British taste for beef had a devastating impact on the impoverished and disenfranchised people of... Ireland... pushed off the best pasture land and forced to farm smaller plots of marginal land, the Irish turned to the potato, a crop that could be grown abundantly in less favorable soil. Eventually, cows took over much of Ireland, leaving the native population virtually dependent on the potato for survival."

Mrs. Gerrard, a large landholder in Galway noted that Irish beef brought more cash than Irish grain and decided to evict her tenant farmers and modernize her estate in 1846 as the hunger from the potato failure was beginning. She enlisted the 49th Regiment, the 13th Regiment, and the police. They marched to the whitewashed cottages of Ballinlass, with their "neat kitchen gardens", on March 13, 1846. The constables and soldiers began to violently dismantle the town with the " screaming of children, the wild wailing of mothers... roofs and walls came tumbling down." By late afternoon the entire village of 270 was destroyed except for an elderly couple's house with fever. The villagers attempted to rebuild their houses with sticks and their landlord had them evicted again and hounded across the countryside by her constables. "Well, God forgive her. She ordered her bailiffs to root up the foundations to prevent the wretches -- its wretches...they were called from going there any more. I saw one ... woman with a child on her breast hunted from three places by the bailiffs."[12]

Prior to this destruction, the residents of Ballinlass had been relatively well off and able to pay their rent - but Mrs. Gerrard could make more money destroying the village for cows. The incident was investigated by Lord Londonderry who reported to the House of Lords,"I am deeply grieved, but there is no doubt concerning the truth of the evictions at Ballinlass. Seventy six families, comprising 300 individuals had not only been turned out of their houses, but had even - the unfortunate wretches - been mercilessly driven from the ditches to which they had been taken themselves for shelter..these unfortunate people had their rents actually ready.."

The potato blight, *Phytophthora Infestans,* is believed to have originated in the Toluca Valley of Mexico. It devastated the potato crop in the eastern US in 1843 -1844. It arrived in Europe and spread rapidly. In 1845 it destroyed between one third and one half the potato crop in Ireland. In 1846 three quarters of the crop was lost. In 1847 less potatoes were planted so the harvest was again small even though the yields had returned to normal. In 1848 the crop was still reduced by one third.

With 3 million Irish completely dependent on the potato for food, it was inevitable that hunger would stalk the land. It was not inevitable that 1.25 million people die and the population be reduced by 25%. The Irish representatives in Parliament largely represented the rich land holders and not the hungry tenant farmers. Taking care of the needs of the Irish population was not the primary objective of the London based parliament.

In November 1845, a deputation of the citizens of Dublin offered suggestions such as opening the ports to the importation of food, banning the export of food, and providing employment through public works. If these steps had been taken it is likely that much of the disaster might have been avoided. Daniel O'Connell pointed out that Belgium had shut down the export of food from Belgium to help Belgium deal with the crisis. Ireland herself had used a similar response in the 18th century. Ireland had previously experienced a famine in 1782-3, and had in response closed the ports to keep Irish food in Ireland to feed the Irish. It had worked- local food prices dropped and the effects of the famine ameliorated. The merchant capitalists had lobbied against this measure, but the government in the 1780's persisted in its successful policy. However, in the 1840's the ideological incorporation of the Free Trade policy preempted taking this logical and humanitarian course. In the nineteenth century the plantations continued to export their cash crops of food. Up to 3/4 of the Irish acreage was planted in wheat, oats, barley for export and shipped abroad while people starved. In 1847, 400,000 Irish men, women, and children died of starvation and starvation related disease. Meanwhile 4000 vessels carried food from Ireland to England. The food was shipped under British military guard.

The British government did try to ameliorate the suffering although not with the intensity that the crisis required. Over the course of the famine the government spent 7,000,000 pounds sterling between 1845 and 1850 - less than one half of one percent of GNP. In the 1830's the government had spent 20,000,000 pounds to compensate West Indian slave owners for the emancipation of their slaves.

John Mitchel in 1860 wrote, "I have called it an artificial famine: that is to say, it was a famine which desolated a rich and fertile island that produced every year abundance and superabundance to sustain all her people and many more. The English, indeed call the famine a 'dispensation of Providence;' and ascribe it entirely to the blight on the potatoes. But the potatoes failed all over Europe; yet there was no famine save in Ireland. The British account of the matter, then, is first, a fraud; second a blasphemy. The Almighty, indeed, sent the potato blight but the English created the famine."

The potato blight was a significant stressor to the structure of Europe contributing in no small way to the revolutions of 1848. However, the catastrophic starvation and depopulation that occurred in Ireland was not replicated elsewhere in Europe. The failure that occurred in a fertile corner of the freest most capitalist country in Europe; it was a failure caused by the incentives being set in such a way that rather than capitalism serving the needs of the population, the population was reduced by 25% to serve the needs of capitalism. 1,250,000 dead is the equivalent of 12 Atomic bombs and is inexcusable. This is a definite failure of Adam Smith's invisible hand to respond humanely to a crisis. The Anglo Irish elite that presided over much of Ireland and held most of her capital were left free to serve their own needs - which they did. It is this class of Anglo Irish gentry that could have ameliorated the suffering the easiest if they had seen that as part of their job description. If they had grown grain or cabbages for domestic consumption to stop the starvation of their tenants there would have been no mass starvation. But they didn't see saving their tenants from starvation as their job description; maximizing return on capital was their lodestone. It is a mistake to moralize about these people being deficient- they may have been but there will be similar deficiencies in capitalists and people until the end of time. (Don't stare too hard at the mirror). Similar events could easily happen again. What was lacking was a political sovereign to take charge, declare a state of emergency, develop a workable plan, and then execute that plan. What instead happened was the landlords used the power of the government to preserve order while they maximized profit. Mrs Gerard could never by herself without the government have destroyed the village of Ballinlass. However, rather than the government compelling Mrs Gerard to take care of her people until the crisis passed, the government assisted Mrs Gerard in the destruction of her tenants.

The twelve richest men landowners in Skibbereen had an annual income of almost £25,000,000 (37,000,000 dollars) in today's money.[13] However, the local newspapers of the winter of 1846 -7 present stories from a Gothic horror tale. *The Cork Examiner* stated that the district is "but a theater for famine, disease, and death. One, two, three, four victims in a hovel. Old women turned into maniacs. The hourly presence of death in every appalling shape has extinguished every human sympathy." A new type of pauper was seen. "A knock is heard at a hall door. Who is it, some poor wretch seeking a morsel of bread? Open it. What!- a starving mother thrusting her dead child before her and begging, not for ...bread, though she is gaunt and fleshless with famine and her eyes roll fearfully- but for a coffin."[14] The rich did not use their economic power to save their neighbors in a time of great distress. The stories of the wretched starving people are gripping: Mr. Cummings, the Cork magistrate, was told Dr Donovan had found seven starving people under the same blanket. One had died but the others were to sick too move the corpse. The police opened a cabin door and found two bodies half eaten by rats. A mother "was seen dragging the corpse of a girl of about twelve" into the middle of the lane where she stopped and began to cover her daughter's "perfectly naked" body with stones.[15] (Eventually there were 1.25 million awful stories).

The next spring the Irish began to flee Ireland en masse. In 1847, 215,000 went to North America and another 150,000 went to England. Only 1/3 of Irishmen born in 1831 would die in their native island of old age.[16] They were shipped to Canada on lumber ships returning from England. Putting these malnourished immunosuppressed people together in the holds of ships designed for carrying boards was a medical disaster. They gave each other typhus and dysentery.

Lord Palmerston made the calculation and realized his estate would be better off financially if the inhabitants left. The first ship he sent across, the *Carricks*, was sunk in the St Lawrence in a May storm killing 87 out of 187 passengers. In June his hired ship the *Eliza Little* arrived with 7 dead, 6 almost dead, and 100 passengers with typhus and dysentery. The *Numa* and the *Marchioness Breadalbane* arrived with 44 dead. The *Aeolus* - hired by Palmerston and his neighbor, Mr. Robert George Booth - arrived in November with 8 dead, 22 dying , and the rest of the 377 passengers sick. On arrival in November when the passengers were mustered on deck for examination they were stark naked except for "blankets and other articles of bedding tied around the waist with rope yarn."[17]

This was not intentionally brutal on Palmerston's part, but there was a complete lack of attention on his part and that of his agents that led to the disaster. This comes from treating people as a number on a sheet of paper, a commodity, rather than as fellow human beings. It also comes from willfully averting one's gaze from one's actions.

Lord Palmerston

Henry John Temple

In addition to being a plantation capitalist, he had a distinguished career in the British government as foreign secretary and Prime Minister. To support Free Trade principles, he was active in setting policy leading to two Opium Wars with China to encourage the Chinese to buy Opium.

8. Donald McLeod, *Donald McLeod's Gloomy memories in the Highlands of Scotland:versus Mrs. Harriet Beecher Stowe's Sunny memories in(England) a foreign land, or, A faithful picture of the extirpation of the Celtic race from the Highlands of Scotland. p8-10.*
9. Ibid., p16 -17.
10. Ibid., p 48 - 49.
11. Ibid., p165 -166.
12. John Kelly, *The Graves are Walking*, (Picador), p 80 -83
13. Ibid., p 193.
14. Ibid., p 191.
15. Ibid., p 194.
16. Ibid., p 256.
17. Ibid., p 284.

The Cell and the Concepts of Homeostasis, the Internal Environment, Boundaries, Control Mechanisms with Positive and Negative Feedback Loops.

The smallest living things are viruses with a small fragment of nucleic acid packaged in a protein coat. Larger viruses have a membrane and a fluid matrix. Larger bacteria have organelles but no nucleus. Higher organisms have a nucleated cell. The nucleus provides a control center for all of the activities of the cell and provides for exact reproduction of the cell.

The tiny viruses are intracellular parasites which can only grow and reproduce in a host cell. As life progresses in complexity and size, there is development of multicellular organisms. This divides the animal (or plant) into different cells each with a nucleus to monitor the function of that cell. A cell membrane defines what is intracellular and what is extracellular. This boundary is critical for life. The nucleus is responsible for what goes on inside the cell. The cell also interacts with the extracellular fluid in a highly regulated fashion.

In the human body, the intracellular concentration of sodium is 10 mEq/l, and the extracellular concentration is 142 mEq/l. The intracellular concentration of potassium is 140 mEq/l, and the extracellular concentration is 4 mEq/l. <u>While it is true that at some point the sodium and potassium inside and outside the cell must come to equilibrium, it should be recognized that at that point the cell will be swollen and dead.</u>

Boundaries are important for life. Boundaries are important for organizations of complex structures because they establish domains of accountability over which a plan can be implemented and responsibility assigned. Neglect of boundaries has led to errors in thinking that have had adverse consequences in economics. It has led to a lack of responsibility among our leaders and the loss of even an expectation of responsibility.

There is a developing consensus among elites that national boundaries are anachronistic and a barrier to the harmonious development of a prosperous world. The modern view of the world has been shaped by many things among which are jet travel, the atomic bomb, and free trade theory. Jet travel has increased mobility tremendously and has made distances seem to shrink. Borders seem to lose their meaning from an ariel view, and an increasing superficial acquaintance with our fellow man abroad makes the need for boundaries less clear. The horrors of 20th century war and the knowledge that an atomic war must be prevented has led (especially in Europe, but also among North American leaders) to the notion that the nation state must be subsumed into a larger entity lest the passions that lurk in the human heart slip their leash and disrupt the peace. Free trade theory and its attendant globalization is based on the idea that everyone benefits as transnational trade is increased. This has absolutely changed the world, with the rapid rise of Asian economies to meet the demands of Western societies. Of course, all of these views have validity, but the removal of boundaries makes other problems unsolvable and diminishes accountability.

The concept of territoriality predates human existence and can be seen with loons selecting nesting sites, fish guarding their nests, and tigers marking their range. The claim that this piece of the planet is mine and if you enter here we will fight is a political/biological statement that goes back millions of years. Walnut trees put toxins into the ground that make the soil less hospitable for other trees. Within his claimed territory an animal can typically reproduce and find food to prosper.

The jaw dropping unwillingness of our leaders to effectively enforce and regulate our boundaries has led to an inability to protect our workers and their families from a world sink of poverty and misery. Products produced by underpaid workers overseas are brought in to underprice our domestic workers. Excess workers from around the world are imported to drive down the wage scale of our workers. Not surprisingly, our inflation adjusted wages have not risen since the 1970's, our birthrate just hit an all time low.

The man in the street looks at his sheep dog and notes that she protects her fence line, protects her young, and protects her dog bowl. This is foreign policy at its most primitive- protecting your land, your children, and your means of sustenance. It should be a checklist as a minimal requirement for any foreign policy. The fact that it is not on our policy makers agenda is almost incomprehensible. It renders the foreign policy establishment so contemptible that no one cares when the media makes fun of a Governor of Alaska for not knowing an arcane point of George Bush's doctrine.

During the Bush presidency the concept of boundary had been eroded to the point where the defense department was outsourcing recruitment of soldiers to Latin America, manufacturing of green beret's to China, and reaching the conclusion that deficits didn't matter. The result this viewpoint can be seen in worsening Trade Balance in the graph below.

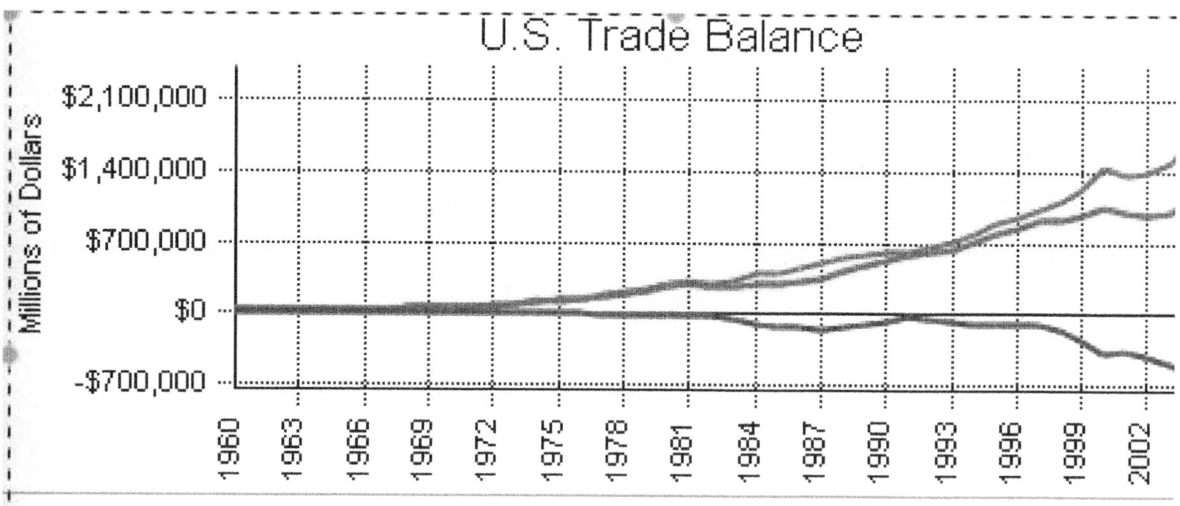

Actual Balance of Payments (U.S. Census Bureau, Foreign Trade Division.)

Total Exports (U.S. Census Bureau, Foreign Trade Division.)

Total Imports (U.S. Census Bureau, Foreign Trade Division.)

www.data360.org

Within a boundary legitimate authority can be established, policies implemented, and the results of these policies judged. A free people have the right to judge policy and change the leaders if the plans that are established are not promoting the general welfare. This typically leads to strong vibrant countries because the leaders have to deliver for the people. A rough scientific experiment is run as people judge if their needs are being met.

Authority established outside the boundary without the representation of those over whom it is established will typically become resented. This is to some extent the definition of empire. It is typically asserted by military means and will often be resisted violently. It is difficult to establish means for extracting revenue from the governed so it will often be a drain of resources from the homeland of the authority. The authority will not be attuned to the needs and wants of the governed and will have difficulty designing graceful policies that meet the needs and wants of the people and at the same time obtaining loyalty of the ruled but not represented population.

To repeat, boundaries are fundamental to the organization of complex structures. When we drive, we drive on the right side of the road. At one level our freedom is constrained by this rule, but at another level it prevents chaos. If Charley hears a voice in his head that tells him he owns the left side of the road and should drive on it, we hope he ends up in the psychiatric ward before the hospital or morgue. Boundaries are fundamental to property rights. Whose land is it? - well, here is plat and the deed and James owns the land on one side of the stone fence and Sarah owns the land on the other side. Once a boundary is established, different things can occur on one side of the boundary from the other. One man may carefully tend his land while a second may neglect his. The separate results establish accountability. This is good because it provides an environment where one's actions have consequences. One's works (or lack thereof) have meaning.

There is always a tension when performance on one side of a boundary is different than on the other. With fluids there is oncotic pressure when the electrolytes are more concentrated on one side than another. When people see that their neighbor's field is well tended and prosperous, they want to become more like him. They will attempt to adapt his methods to their own field. If, over time, they cannot close the gap resentment will begin to grow and they will want to expropriate the better life on the other side of the boundary for themselves.

Inequalities across boundaries will serve as an inducement to trade as two different environments will have comparative advantages and comparative weaknesses. Entrepreneurs will seek to exploit this tension for profit. They will lobby to facilitate trade to increase their profits. This trade will diminish the differences across the boundary. This may or may not be good for the citizens of the countries involved - if, for example, the English are bringing opium into China as happened in the 19th century this would likely have a deleterious affect on Chinese society. (Actually cartels bringing cocaine into the United States are not beneficial to us either). Countries have an interest in maintaining a stable internal environment and regulating trade and keeping the border intact is a critical aspect of this.

Humans are cellular animals. That is to say, every person is composed of roughly 75 trillion separate cells harmoniously working together. Each of these cells lives and draws its sustenance from the extracellular fluid, and each cell in turn contributes to the well being of the individual. 56% of the human body is fluid. Approximately 1/3 is extracellular and 2/3 is intracellular. The extracellular fluid is known as the internal milieu (a term introduced by the 19th century French physiologist Claude Bernard). This is the internal environment of the body. Maintaining this internal milieu at optimal conditions is crucial for cellular survival and function. These are measured by your physician when he assesses your health. If they are out of the normal range he will go looking for a cause because that is an indication of malfunction.
A partial listing of the values follows:

Albumin 3.5 - 5.0 gm/dl
Bilirubin, direct 0.0 - 0.4 mg/dl
Bilirubin, total 0.2 - 1.4 mg/dl
BUN 6 - 23 mg/dl
Calcium 8 - 11 mg/dl
Carbon Dioxide 21 - 34 mEq/L
Creatinine 0.6 - 1.5 mg/dl
Glucose 65 - 99 mg/dl
Potassium 3.5 - 5.5 mEq/L
Sodium 135 - 148 mEq/L

Total Protein 5 - 9 gm / dl
Blood Urea Nitrogen 8 - 25 mg/dl

It is not by accident that these blood chemistries are maintained within the above ranges. There are a wide variety of control mechanisms that function to do this. Physiologists call the maintenance of a static, constant, optimal internal environment *homeostasis.*

Cells are dependent on the extracellular fluid being maintained with optimal concentrations of oxygen, glucose, electrolytes, protein substrates, etc. The organs and tissues of the body operate in such a way as to maintain these constant conditions. The stomach and gut absorb nutrients from the outside world and dispose of useless material. The kidneys monitor and maintain the extracellular fluid of the blood and keep the blood serum in satisfactory balance by eliminating excess electrolytes, water, and urea. The liver provides a wide variety of metabolic functions such as eliminating toxins, storing glycogen, etc. The lungs absorb oxygen and eliminate CO2. The heart and circulatory system transport the metabolites to the various organs so they can function. The brain, eyes, and muscles function to allow the body to procure food and to avoid being squashed by a truck.

Similarly, governments of a free people are instituted to provide a peaceful, just, happy environment for people to live in. The maintenance of an internal environment where people can found a family and economically prosper is essential for a lasting society. The preamble to the United States Constitution speaks to these needs. "We, the people of the United States, in Order to form a more perfect Union, establish Justice, insure the domestic Tranquility, provide for the common defense, promote the general Welfare, and secure the Blessings of Liberty of ourselves and our Posterity, do ordain and establish this Constitution for the United States of America." Roughly translated- We are going to cooperate to avoid intramural conflict and be more secure from external conflict, and we are going to cooperate to provide a just, free, prosperous society for our members. Or as a physiologist would describe it, we are going to cooperate to provide a stable internal environment where our citizens can prosper- we are going to maintain homeostasis in our internal milieu. Maintenance of this homeostatic environment in the face of external threats and internal stresses is the job of government.

The human body faces analogous issues. It interacts with the external world and internal environment in ways to maintain the extracellular fluid in a state to promote optimal functioning of the cells. The interactions with the external world tend to be more conscious - driving a car, calling a friend on the phone, instructing a child. The interactions with the internal environment are less conscious - the stomach and intestine digesting food, the heart pumping blood, the kidneys filtering the blood, the maintenance of a constant body temperature.

These unconscious interactions by and large are controlled by negative feedback loops. The hemoglobin molecule is designed to release its oxygen if the concentration of oxygen has fallen too low but holds onto the oxygen if the oxygen concentration is adequate. This release of oxygen where concentration is too low maintains homeostasis by preferentially distributing oxygen to the hypoxic regions of the body. Carbon dioxide, an exhaust gas of the body, needs to be removed to prevent toxicity. High carbon dioxide levels trigger the respiratory center of the brain to increase the respiratory rate which reduces the carbon dioxide level. The kidneys respond to too low a sodium level

by holding onto sodium; they respond to too high a potassium level by dumping potassium. When you eat too much you are satiated and stop eating. When you are dehydrated, your brain (hypothalamus) makes you thirsty so you drink. When you
work out and get hot, you will perspire to dissipate the heat.

Positive feedback loops, on the other hand, do not cause homeostasis but are disruptive. Positive feedback loops can be a cause of death. One common way to die is multi system failure, where failure of one organ(say the heart) leads to failure of the kidneys to excrete fluid, which leads to pulmonary congestion (fluid building up in the lung)and poor lung function. This causes hypoxia which leads to worsening cardiac function in vicious cycle.

In human behavior, people tend to respond to a positive feedback loop by trying more of the same. This is why it is so dangerous to win when gambling, because the tendency is to up the bet. Napoleon and Hitler kept increasing the scope of their wars until they encountered catastrophic failure. This is of course a large part of the business cycle- people are rewarded for an activity and focus their energy in that direction until the market is saturated. Then there is a collapse with failure which serves as negative feedback pushing the system towards a dynamic equilibrium. Because the world is finite, a positive feedback loop tends to lead to an increase in the activity until another force countervails - often with severe and discontinuous consequences.

Capitalism is a positive feedback cycle. If you make money as an entrepreneur you will grow and have more resources to deploy. We see this process in the Parable of the Talents:

Matthew 25:14-30English Standard Version (ESV)
The Parable of the Talents
14 “For it will be like a man going on a journey, who called his
servants[a] and entrusted to them his property. **15** To one he

gave five talents,[b] to another two, to another one, to each
according to his ability. Then he went away. **16** He who had
received the five talents went at once and traded with them,
and he made five talents more. **17** So also he who had the
two talents made two talents more. **18** But he who had
received the one talent went and dug in the ground and hid
his master's money. **19** Now after a long time the master of
those servants came and settled accounts with them. **20** And
he who had received the five talents came forward, bringing
five talents more, saying, 'Master, you delivered to me five
talents; here I have made five talents more.' **21** His master
said to him, 'Well done, good and faithful servant.[c] You have
been faithful over a little; I will set you over much. Enter into
the joy of your master.' **22** And he also who had the two
talents came forward, saying, 'Master, you delivered to me
two talents; here I have made two talents more.' **23** His
master said to him, 'Well done, good and faithful servant. You
have been faithful over a little; I will set you over much. Enter
into the joy of your master.' **24** He also who had received the
one talent came forward, saying, 'Master, I knew you to be a
hard man, reaping where you did not sow, and gathering
where you scattered no seed, **25** so I was afraid, and I went
and hid your talent in the ground. Here you have what is
yours.' **26** But his master answered him, 'You wicked and
slothful servant! You knew that I reap where I have not sown
and gather where I scattered no seed? **27** Then you ought to
have invested my money with the bankers, and at my coming
I should have received what was my own with interest. **28** So
take the talent from him and give it to him who has the ten
talents. **29** For to everyone who has will more be given, and
he will have an abundance. But from the one who has not,
even what he has will be taken away. **30** And cast the
worthless servant into the outer darkness. In that place there
will be weeping and gnashing of teeth.'

The resources flow to the servants who make money and away from the wretch who was just trying to save. This is a positive feedback loop.

Mathematically, a process that grows exponentially like capitalism will exhaust any finite domain. It is inherently disruptive. One can predict a capitalist cycle. Initially, a new technology such as tractor manufacturing is developed. There are many entrants into the field. The better companies thrive and expand rapidly. Soon, competition ensues and increases . Many companies go out of business. Others adapt to changing conditions by altering what they do. Eventually about 3-4 companies remain, competition abates, growth slows, and a more steady state business ensues.

This leads to a major and ancient problem of statecraft. <u>How can you have a stable economy - a stable internal environment - when the driving force of your economy- capitalism - is an intrinsically disruptive process?</u> Here are several approaches:

1. Recognize that capitalism is intrinsically unstable and therefore not a fixed star to steer by. It is more like a gasoline explosion. Contained and regulated it can power a car or plane. Uncontrolled it can be wildly destructive like refinery fire or Napalm. A good starting point is to maintain as your objective the happiness and well being of society - the internal milieu - rather than a search for always maximizing profit. This was shown in Chapter 2 by contrasting the experience of the Massachusetts Bay Colony which was undertaken for religious reasons with the sad experience of Barbados which was all about the money - no one would ever say that Massachusetts was not commercial - but that wasn't her central reason for being. Concentrate on providing a stable environment where people are valued and raised right and many of them will find ideas about which to found a business. (A similar pattern can be seen in the Mormon experience in Utah where the main focus is centered on the family and religion, but which has in no small way had a pattern of commercial success.)

2. Follow the central bank Keynesian strategy of leaning against the wind. Adopt more stimulative policies when the economy is slow and more constrictive policies when things take off. A negative feedback loop that restricts capitalism could in theory restrain the positive cascade and lead to a more damped business cycle.

3. Use trade barriers so the entire world doesn't have a simultaneous downturn.

4. Embrace the concept of small. Knowing that we are dealing with an explosive process, lets figure out how to use it appropriately. What we want with Capitalism is to organize our society so our best leaders structure our efforts in a fruitful way that allows everyone to prosper according to their ability and willingness to work. We want to incorporate scientific advances and to allow our leaders of genius to execute their artistic visions. Encouraging dinosaur corporation creation that exists because of its size does little to unlock the genius of our people. In particular, the creation of banking institutions that are deemed too big to fail is guaranteed to suck vitality away from more vibrant parts of society. The failure of a small enterprise will not greatly disrupt the internal milieu of society provided that it isn't synchronized with more systemic failure elsewhere. Smaller firms encourage more competition and innovation. They are also less likely to corrupt the system and have less opportunity to become practice monopolistic business practices.

To return to our gasoline analogy, it is 229 miles from New York to Washington, DC. At roughly 30 miles per gallon in a 4 cylinder hypothetical Honda that would be 7.3 gallons. If an individual were to dump 7.3 gallons in a garbage can and attempt to use the explosion to blow him to Washington we would think the notion absurd and reckless on its face. But to carefully burn that same gas in a 4 hour drive we would have every expectation of an uneventful drive. To accomplish this we have divided our 7.3 gallon explosion into 4 hours x 60 minutes/ hour x 60 seconds / minute x 2000 cycles / second x 4 cylinders explosions = 115.2 million explosions. When divided into small events the drive doesn't have an explosive nature - just the satisfying whine of the engine. All of these explosions take place in the bounds of a cylinder and are used purposefully.

5. Strive to have a diversified economy. Different industries, and businesses will have different moments of strength and weakness. This will serve to damp the more dynamic ends of the business cycle.

6. Recognize that failure will occur. Bankruptcy should let our people be free after a short sojourn in poverty, not be a permanently disabling condition. In a Democratic society, as Pericles said, "To avow poverty with us is no disgrace, the true disgrace is in doing nothing to avoid it." When we have systemic failure a form of a year of Jubilee with debt forgiveness may be warranted.

7. Be wary of foreign large capitalist firms which are strong enough to destabilize your country so they do not set up an exploitive form of capitalism.

8. Recognize that firms that originally were native to your country may take on characteristics of large foreign firms as they grow and become global entities.

9. Discourage debt. Mistakes made with cash are less debilitating for the future. A society that is debt free is to a large extent free, a society that is in debt much less so.

Any comparison of capitalism and biology would be incomplete without a discussion of Darwin's Theory of Evolution and the creative destruction of capitalism. In biology, an organism exists in an environmental niche and competes for survival with other organisms in that same niche. A new gene (idea) may have a positive, neutral, or negative competitive advantage. Most genetic changes if they lead to expressed traits will have a negative competitive advantage (These could range from "Dude you look slightly different." to "Dude, you are abnormal." to "Dude, there is really something wrong with you." to "Dude, you are already dead.") Those genes with a negative selective advantage are eliminated or decreased in the population. If on the other hand the gene (idea) leads to a greater chance for survival of the organism in that environment, the gene will be increased in the population. Sometimes the gene (idea) will allow the organism to enter a new environment and compete in a new arena. Continuous competition decreases or eliminates the bad or less useful genes in favor of the more useful genes.

Capitalism at its best allows an entrepreneur to take an idea and make a profit from it. If he is successful he will by reinvesting his profits grow his business exponentially. With access to credit and capital markets he can grow his business even faster. A successful idea will rapidly invite competition in the form of imitators. This will also propagate the idea. Thus capitalism has the ability to lead to the rapid adaptation and implementation of new ideas. This is often a huge benefit for society. It also leads to rapid change and internal creative stress.

Often a gifted capitalist leader will implement a variety of useful ideas in the course of his career - perhaps the most obvious example would be Thomas Edison although the list is long and would include Henry Ford, Henry J Kaiser, Steve Jobs, and Sam Walton to name a few. Elevating talented men to positions of power, motivating them to make society better, and rewarding them with additional power to improve society when they succeed is one of the geniuses of capitalism. Giving negative feedback when leaders are less talented, less driven, less motivated, less intelligent, less organized, less competitive by reducing the scope of their activities is also good for society's well being.

Capitalism is also all about the organization, the enterprise. A capitalist leader will have to motivate his work force to be competitive, and his work force will reflect his spirit. When Adam Smith writes of the working class of English and Dutch towns who are supported by capital being industrious, sober, and thriving, it is to no small extent because their leaders willed them to be. They have to be; you can't run a competitive enterprise with idle, dissolute, losers. Thus if you can maximize employment in a capitalist society, you will to some extent create a more virtuous society, because the behaviors that make for a useful worker also make for a better citizen. Idle hands are definitely the Devil's workshop. Or, to quote Colonel Sanders, "A man will rust out before he will wear out."

Archetypes of Capitalism

Anglo Saxon Capitalism (Liberal Capitalism)

The Golden Rule: He who has the Gold makes the Rules.

This is the form of unfettered laissez faire capitalism espoused by Adam Smith (although much is done under this rubric that he would likely denounce if he were here to see it). The theory is that in a free economy where people are left alone by the government, they will pursue their own interests, and that by pursuing their own interests they will do not only the most good for themselves, but for society. This will bring about a prosperous and happy society.

> "But the annual revenue of every society is always precisely equal to the exchangeable value of the whole annual produce of its industry, or rather is precisely the same thing with that exchangeable value. As every individual, therefore, endeavors as much as he can both to employ his capital in the support of domestic industry, and so to direct that industry that its produce may be of the greatest value, every individual necessarily labors to render the annual revenue of the society as great as he can. He generally, indeed, neither intends to promote the public interest, nor knows how much he is promoting it. By preferring the support of domestic to that of foreign industry, he intends only his own security; and by directing that industry in such a manner as its produce may be of the greatest value, he

intends only his own gain, and he is in this, as in many other cases, led by an **invisible hand** to promote an end which was no part of his intention. Nor is it always the worse for the society that it was not part of it. By pursuing his own interest he frequently promotes that of the society more effectually than when he really intends to promote it. I have never known much good done by those who affected to trade for the public good. It is an affectation, indeed, not very common among merchants, and very few words need be employed in dissuading them from it."

- Adam Smith Book IV, Chapter II, paragraph IX of *The Wealth of Nations*.

Basically this form of capitalism advocates allowing each person to do as he wills and the free market will allocate resources and effort to those issues where the greatest human needs will be met and the greatest human accomplishment achieved. The market will give continuous feedback as to whether an endeavor should be pursued or not. Smith described his world of rapid progress due to the industrial revolution and division of labor with respect for the dramatic steps of human progress that were being made. He acutely observed his world and his time.

According to this model of Capitalism, profit isn't the main thing, it is the only thing. However, in theory, profits are connected to social utility. As above, Smith correctly said that <u>frequently</u> the entrepreneur promotes the general welfare when he is only seeking a personal profit. This is of course true. Smith does not say this is <u>always</u> the case, but Free Market enthusiasts express a faith in this invisible hand when promoting Anglo Saxon capitalism. They are making a case further than the evidence allows. You can hypothesize a beneficent invisible hand as the optimal instrument of growth when your pattern of capitalism is producing fruits you find pleasing, as in Adam Smith's day. That is no longer logical when the results are poor. Looking at the historical record, there are several glaring problems with this model of capitalism:

1) Underperformance of the English economy since 1890.

The English economy was outperformed by Germany following German unification under Bismarck in the 1870 Franco Prussian War. Some of this was due to tariffs imposed by Germany, some of it was due to catch up by the Germans, and certainly other factors could be involved. The United States also had a relatively closed economy (tariff protected) compared with Great Britain and also outperformed the British. There has also been significant underperformance of the English economy since WWII versus the German economy. Scientifically when you repeat an experiment and you repeatedly fail, it might be time to reconsider your hypothesis.

2) Lack of a theory of effective demand.

Adam Smith did not discuss demand in his work. Ricardo side-stepped the issue- "Political Economy you think is an enquiry into the nature and causes of wealth- I think it should be called an enquiry into the laws which determine the division of the produce of industry amongst the classes who concur in its formation. No law can be laid down respecting quantity, but a tolerably correct one can be laid down respecting proportions. Every day I am more satisfied that the former enquiry is vain and delusive, and the latter only the only true objects of the science." Letter to Malthus of October 9, 1820 from Page 4, The General Theory of Employment, Interest, and Money, John Maynard Keynes.

3) Plantation Capitalism.

Plantation Capitalism, where capitalists make their margin by pushing down the wage scale, has led to severe human disasters in the past. More salient, it is the general business plan of Free Market capitalists today and is currently leading to oppression of working / middle classes in developed countries and huge deflationary pressures.

4) Underperformance of the American economy since 1973. Wages (inflation adjusted) in the US economy have been stagnant/ slowly declining for the past 40 years. 40 years of failure is enough. QED.

If for a period of time a shoemaker carefully cuts out leather for shoes, and every night they are assembled into beautiful shoes while he sleeps, it might make sense for the shoemaker to stay up and see if there are magical elves with invisible hands helping him. If, on the other hand, for forty years a shoemaker carefully cuts out leather for shoes, and wakes up every morning and has to assemble them on his own, it would be the height of folly to expect the elves to show up next week to take him to the top of the shoemaking world.

5) Lack of corporate accountability. Lack of the world of finance to behave responsibly towards main street.

The corporation is set up not to have normal accountability. The CEO's interest may differ from the shareholders leading to unwarranted stock options. There are other ways that the corporation can be looted contrary to the interest of the owners. Two quotes from Keynes illustrate this. "Experience is accumulating that remoteness between ownership and operation is an evil in the relations among men, likely or certain in the long run to set up strains and enmities which will bring to nought the financial calculation." "When the same principal is applied internationally it is, in times of stress, intolerable. I am irresponsible towards what I own, and those who operate what I own are irresponsible towards me."

Adam Smith thought the corporations of his day were not well run and would be surprised and dismayed by their dominance today.

6) Corruption of governments around the world. Crony capitalism.

7) Environmental law.
There is the possibility that in various endeavors (mining comes to mind), the profits may be concentrated but the costs distributed to the general society. This ability of a business entity to cause general mayhem while making a profit needs to be addressed by governmental policy (or it simply won't be addressed and mayhem will ensue- things fall apart).
8) Lack of any discussion for the need for antitrust legal framework. The historical record shows that capitalism is cumulative. This is in many ways good because it puts capital in capable hands initially. However, there are downsides. After the initial winnowing process, companies may survive by being big rather than being great which can suppress other companies with good ideas but insufficient capital. Also large corporations are bad for democracy because they will get laws passed that favor them. This tends to push political power away from the people.

9) Poorer management on the shop floor.
The top down organization flowing from the treatment of workers as commodities to be hired and fired rather than long term partners in a productive enterprise renders the US and UK models of capitalism vulnerable to competition from models that more carefully manage their workforces. When workers are made expendable and are not respected, the quality of their output is reduced. Low expectations breed low performance. Further, bottom up insights are lost/ ignored leading to mistakes and waste. It is difficult to create a learning organization without respecting the workers. The organization will learn little from the workers it disrespects. It can still learn from those workers and consultants that it does respect, but from those that it commoditizes, it will learn little.

All of these subjects could be discussed at length. Since this is an overview a very superficial discussion is given.

Adam Smith

1723-1790
Author of *Theory of Moral Sentiments* and *The Wealth of Nations*

Plantation Capitalism

Plantation Capitalism is where the business owner thinks chiefly of his workers as a commodity, an object, an expense to be minimized. The classic example is slavery, but this was a further progression of a mindset toward labor that was already in place in the plantations in Ireland. Typically in plantation capitalism there is a mindset towards pushing down salaries, searching the world for the cheapest source of labor, and having no loyalty towards labor.

In North America, where free or cheap land was abundant until the closing of the frontier (see Frederick Jackson Turner 1893), free labor always had the option of going West. This set a base value on labor below which free labor could not be oppressed. For a plantation owner to extract greater value from his holdings than his neighbor, he had to control his labor costs. Sugar cane, tobacco, and cotton all were labor intensive crops which made slavery the cheapest form of labor. In the North, the grain crops were more seasonal which made free labor cheaper since you weren't responsible for the worker when he wasn't working which was most of the time. Slavery was able to cast its long grim shadow across the South because a farm run on slavery had lower costs than a farm run on free hired labor, and was therefore more profitable and more likely to grow. It could out compete farms run on hired labor. Individual farmers farming their own land could also exist on the labor of the farmer and his family so the South was not a monolithic slave society, but the large farms tended to run on slavery. Paradoxically, the slave states that could provide the largest number of troops in the Civil War were those states with large numbers of small yeoman farmers. The mindset of denigrating labor spilled over from the slave who was the bottom to the small farmer who was termed "poor white trash".

The small farmers did not like the slave economy and many dealt with it by moving away. Abraham Lincoln's family migrated from the South to Indiana to escape slavery (Both of his parents were from Virginia and he was born in Kentucky). Southern Ohio, Indiana, and Illinois were largely settled initially by Virginians and other small Southern farmers. What they were fleeing was the degradation of labor by the moneyed interests.

Slavery did not make for a more well managed part of the country. Along the Ohio river it was noted how much better managed the farms were on the North side of the river in Ohio and Indiana than in Kentucky. Pennsylvania farms were more carefully tended than those in Virginia. The invisible hand of Plantation capitalism, where you take the pride of work from the laborers, does not make for a happier more productive society.

As economic relationships became more complicated with the industrial revolution, free labor could no longer abide slavery. This led to the Civil War and the destruction of slavery. ("Small Fisted Farmers, Mudsills of Society, Greasy Mechanics for A. Lincoln."- campaign banner 1860 election.)[1]

The mindset of Plantation Capitalism, however, lives on in business owners everywhere who wish to lower costs by reducing wages. Bringing in cheap immigrant labor to drive down wages of farm workers is an obvious example of Plantation Capitalism. It is directly analogous to sourcing cheap labor from Africa three hundred and fifty years ago, and to sourcing cheap labor from Africa two hundred years ago. Bringing in cheap labor to drive down the wages in meat packing (by 45%), construction, and trucking strongly echoes this pattern of behavior. Moving textile, furniture, and computer jobs to sweat shops around the world is a similar action.

Anglo Saxon capitalism has been described as a maritime trading capitalism which grew from corporations having a boat, pulling into a port, making deals, and then leaving with a profit with no expectation of an ongoing relationship. (See Phillip Martin's paper, Anglo-Saxon versus Rhenish model capitalism: As different as land and sea., April 2, 2013)

Plantation Capitalism is a variant of Anglo Saxon Capitalism. It has several elements:

1) It is a for profit operation. It is not about community development.

2) Labor is sourced from wherever it is cheapest, like copper or iron.

3) Labor is not valued highly since it is cheap and there is a psychological chasm between labor and ownership and management.

4) In its worst form, Extractive Plantation Capitalism, there is absentee ownership who value the operation solely for the cash flow.

5) Labor is not developed. Training of labor is limited.

6) The market is not the workers. The less the workers consume, the better.

7) Often the the workers and the owners do not pray together. (The Irish Catholics and the English Protestants, the African Methodist Episcopal Church and the Methodists, etc.)

8) There is often a racial ethnic nature of the Plantation Capitalism. In the Ulster Plantation, Calvinist Protestants were

brought in to keep the native Catholic Irish in check. In Barbados, African slaves were brought in but a cadre of "poor whites" were retained to preserve the large landowners' power to intimidate the slaves. Neither the poor whites or the slaves were respected of course.

Initially Plantation Capitalists used racism as an excuse to treat their African workers brutally and created distance between the free workers and the slaves so the common interests of workers could be suppressed. Today, Plantation Capitalists, in a form of jujitsu, use the language of diversity to obscure the fact they are bringing in cheap labor to destroy the wage scale and increase their margins.

9) It runs on fear and greed. There is often a militarized violent undertone.

Plantation Capitalism needs several things to thrive.

1) It needs a market- an external market. Since the workers are oppressed and underpaid, it needs an external market. It is not a complete system since it needs an external market.

2) It needs access to cheap workers. In a closed, wealthy society, it costs too much to hire a worker to not try to maximize his potential as a human and as a worker.

3) It needs psychological distance between the workers and the owners. Given time, the workers and the owners will form a better more egalitarian society if this psychological distance is breached. The relationships between house slaves and field hands and their masters were quite different.

Plantation Capitalism is always an assault on labor. The premise is to search for the world cheap labor and exploit its cheapness to have a profit margin. It thrives on pain whether it is Africans selling Africans to New Englanders, New Englanders selling slaves to Southern Plantations, Okies trying to cope with the dust bowl and depression, or Mexican farmers displaced by NAFTA. There are ways to stop it. You can have a Civil War to stop slavery. You can shut off your markets to goods made with desperately poor labor. And you can stop importing people to drive down the price of labor. What is termed "Free Trade" can have significant costs such an inability to raise wages and an 18.2 trillion dollar deficit.

<u>The sovereign should, at a minimum, recognize that the consumption of society is largely determined by the salaries of these same workers, and when you destroy their wage scale, not only do you demoralize the majority of your population, but also you destroy demand which will shortly destroy production.</u>

Extractive Plantation Capitalism

Plantation Capitalism, as above, describes the state of an entrepreneur making his margin by oppressing/commoditizing labor. To an extent this is less bad for society if he lives in the same place as his work and spends the money locally. In Extractive Plantation Capitalism, on the other hand, the wealth is geographically sent elsewhere and spent elsewhere.

This is in large part a question of where are the profits spent. If they are spent locally, George may make more money by underpaying Frank, but the same money will be spent locally buying extra shoes for George's wife rather than buying shoes for Frank's children. Either way, if we are simply transferring a modest sum to the entrepreneur (Plantation Capitalist) from his work force, and if the Plantation Capitalist spends his money on consumption, the locality around the business is stimulated (Jason the shoemaker is happy selling shoes to George's wife or Frank's children). If, on the other hand, the profits from oppressing Frank are shipped elsewhere, the stimulation to the economy from those profits being spent happens elsewhere.

A classic example of this would be colonial Spain which extracted vast wealth from the New World working many native populations under miserable/genocidal conditions. Rather than this vast wealth flowing to enrich the people of Peru, it was loaded up on a Treasure Fleet and brought back to Spain which became rich and powerful because of it. This allowed Spain to finance a variety of wars including the Armada. (A parallel can perhaps be seen with President Carlos Salinas de Gortari taking billions from Mexico and moving to Ireland- actually extractive corruption).

Thus if our Barbados entrepreneur lives in Barbados and spends his money there, it is just Plantation Capitalism. However, if he moves back to England leaving his estate in the hands of an overseer, joins Parliament, and spends his money in the City of London, it is Extractive Plantation Capitalism. Lord Palmerston living in London and depopulating his Irish estate to improve his cash flow is an example of Extractive Plantation Capitalism. So is the Duchess of Sutherland living in London giving to charities while her overseers genocide her Highland subjects.

Our Southern Founding Fathers (Washington, Jefferson, Madison, Monroe) were Plantation Capitalists, but they lived in America and were not Extractive Plantation Capitalists. This is almost by definition- Extractive Plantation Capitalist from the time would have almost certainly been Tories.

There are several effects of the distance, all of them draining of vitality:

1. The first of course is the economic stimulation from spending the profits is not available locally and this has a depressing effect on local business.

2. The second is that the owner has increased psychological distance from his workers and does not therefore have the human compassion that close personal association will often develop in people who work and live together.

3. The third is by being remote the owner may not (probably will not) run his business as effectively as if he were on location. This can lead to lower profits which a plantation capitalist will try to make up for by oppressing his charges more.

4. The fourth is more intangible but real. The Plantation Capitalists as a class are the talented people who are supposed to be the leaders of their communities. If they are on location they will see opportunities to develop their community and found businesses to meet the needs that are apparent. If they are elsewhere their leadership which is desired is absent. Further, the Plantation Capitalists by extracting the money from the community make it difficult for those who might have a useful insight to act on it (people who

would otherwise act as forces for good feel/are disempowered).

Sugar Estate, Barbados.

Midwestern Capitalism / Fordism.

Henry Ford.

Midwestern Capitalism is capitalism which seeks to profit by developing and organizing its workers to be productive and have pride in that production themselves. It recognizes that each worker is also a consumer. It goes some distance towards recognizing that each worker is a fellow human being and not just a number on a balance sheet that needs to be reduced.

It is called Midwestern Capitalism in honor of Henry Ford, whose bright vision of what capitalism should be is in contrast to the dark world of the plantation. Ford introduced the Model T in 1908 with the aim of making a car cheap enough the masses could buy it. He is widely credited with inventing the assembly the assembly line but the truth is even more to the point. He led a learning organization whose employees Clarence Avery, Peter Martin, Charles Sorensen, and C. Harold Wills formulated the idea of moving a product through multiple workstations - the assembly line. Working as an empowered team, these men solved the problems of mass production. On a Sunday in Detroit in 1910 Sorenson towed a chassis with a rope over his shoulders through the Ford Plant to test his idea. Other workers added the parts. In 1913 Ford introduced moving assembly belts into his factories. The result of this campaign for improvement was skyrocketing sales and falling prices.

The price on a Model T fell from $ 825 in 1908 to $ 360 in

1916. By the 1920's a majority of American drivers had learned to drive on a Model T.

In 1914 Ford raised the salary of his workers to $5 per day which more than doubled their salaries. This enabled him get and keep the best workers in Detroit. It also enabled them to buy the cars they were producing. At one level paying employees well is a sign of respect. Respecting your employees as people is a central theme of Midwestern Capitalism. Companies that place a high value on their employees, and empower their employees are practicing Midwestern Capitalism. Philosophically making a social pact with employees that if they work hard and are loyal to the company, the company will not dump them at the first opportunity to cut costs is fundamental to this.

At a macroeconomic level, Midwestern Capitalism is about paying workers enough to have a good life. This makes for better workers, better factories, and better products, better lives. It also has the potential to be a self contained economic system, because the workers are paid enough to buy the products, unlike plantation capitalism, where the workers are paid meager wages. While at the level of an individual business it sounds radical to pay your workers more, for a society to achieve greatness it is necessary. A higher paid more motivated and more carefully managed workforce will lead to better business practices and will unlock the potential of a society far more than oppressing the workers. Paying workers enough to buy products creates demand for the creative skill and artistic talents of a society so that rather trying to survive on potatoes people can go to the opera, buy new fashion, and learn to fly airplanes. Or whatever they want to do. Having a good life is a good thing.

This is also a stronger society. In crisis, this higher level of consumption can be diverted into the sinew of war. The US auto industry won World War II burying the Axis with planes, bombs, tanks, armaments, and munitions. The production levels weren't even close. Japan had 10 aircraft carriers, we built 100. Germany built 9000 Panzer IV, 4500 Panther, and

1350 Tiger tanks, the USA produced over 40,000 Sherman tanks. Ford's Willow run plant was producing a B-24 Liberator bomber every 58 minutes.

In the 1860's of course, Midwestern Capitalism buried Plantation Capitalism because the African American portion of the South had no motivation to fight for the defense of the system that oppressed them.

Stabilizing the workforce and having a loyal workforce is vital to implementing many of the lean processes in the Toyota in the Toyota Production System. It takes an empowered worker to stop the line when something is wrong. It takes empowered workers to create a learning organization.

Walter A Walter A Shewhart was born on March 18, 1891 in New Canton, Illinois. He received a PHD in physics from the University of California, Berkeley in 1917. He went to work at the Western Electric Company at the Hawthorne Works in Cicero, Illinois in 1918. At that time industrial quality control consisted of inspecting finished products and removing the defective items. On May 16, 1924, according to his boss, George Edwards, "Dr. Shewhart prepared a little memorandum only about a page in length. About a third of that page was given over to a simple diagram we would all recognize today as a schematic control chart. That diagram, and the short text which preceded and followed it, set forth all of the essential principles and considerations which are involved in what we know today as process quality control."

Shewhart invented the Shewhart cycle, also known as the Deming cycle (for W. Edwards Deming who popularized it- and was working with Shewart). This is an iterative management paradigm for continuous quality improvement. The cycle consists four verbs in order. Plan, Do, Check, Act, then repeat. To execute on this takes motivated workers and management that are interested in learning. To do it well takes excellent communication in an organization. This is much more likely to occur in a social and company environment practicing Midwestern Capitalism than in a company and society practicing Plantation Capitalism. It is no accident that when Boeing develops worse relationships with its home workers and then moves factories elsewhere for the purpose of lowering salaries it begins to develop quality problems.

W. Edwards Deming was born in Sioux City, Iowa in 1900 and grew up in Iowa and Wyoming with training as an electrical engineer and mathematical physics. He popularized and expanded upon Shewhart's work. Deming codified part of what he was teaching in his 14 points for quality improvement. Deming developed improved methods for management and leadership that have had a profound effect on how businesses interested in quality are structured.
This is discussed in his classic book, Out of Crisis, (1982) .

The 14 Points.

1. Create constancy of purpose toward improvement of product and service, with the aim to become competitive and to stay in business, and to provide jobs.

2. Adopt the new philosophy. We are in a new economic age. Western management must awaken to the challenge, must learn their responsibilities, and take on leadership for change.

3. Cease dependence on inspection to achieve quality.

Eliminate the need for inspection on a mass basis by building quality into the product in the first place.

4. End the practice of awarding business on the basis of price tag. Instead, minimize total cost. Move toward a single supplier for any one item, on a long-term relationship of loyalty and trust.

5. Improve constantly and forever the system of production and service, to improve quality and productivity, and thus constantly decrease costs.

6. Institute training on the job.

7. Institute leadership (see Point 12 and Ch. 8). The aim of supervision should be to help people and machines and gadgets to do a better job. Supervision of management is in need of overhaul, as well as supervision of production workers.

8. Drive out fear, so that everyone may work effectively for the company (see Ch. 3).

9. Break down barriers between departments. People in research, design, sales, and production must work as a team, to foresee problems of production and in use that may be encountered with the product or service.

10. Eliminate slogans, exhortations, and targets for the work force asking for zero defects and new levels of productivity. Such exhortations only create adversarial relationships, as the bulk of the causes of low quality and low productivity belong to the system and thus lie beyond the power of the work force.

Eliminate work standards (quotas) on the factory floor. Substitute leadership.
Eliminate management by objective. Eliminate management

by numbers, numerical goals. Substitute leadership.

11. Remove barriers that rob the hourly worker of his right to pride of workmanship. The responsibility of supervisors must be changed from sheer numbers to quality.

12. Remove barriers that rob people in management and in engineering of their right to pride of workmanship. This means, inter alia, abolishment of the annual or merit rating and of management by objective (see Ch. 3).

13. Institute a vigorous program of education and self-improvement.

14. Put everybody in the company to work to accomplish the transformation. The transformation is everybody's job.

(The interested reader is referred to The W. Edwards Deming Institute at www.deming.org).

•

•

Photos courtesy of The W. Edwards Deming Institute®. •

• Deming brought his ideas of quality improvement to Japan in the post war period and made a significant contribution to the Japanese post war economic miracle. You can't easily implement these concepts without empowering your workers. To do this well, you need long standing respectful relationships between workers and management. You also

•

• need long relationships with suppliers. In fact, the Toyota Production System is also known as the Respect for Humanity System. In clear contrast, the Plantation System could be termed the Disrespect for Humanity System.

Midwestern Capitalism has several elements:
1. It is a for profit operation.
2. It is also about community development because the workers are paid a good wage.
3. It is about product development because its people are paid enough to buy something if it has value. It assembles people in purposeful teams to solve problems.
4. It is about people development with an educated progressive workforce. The general level of education is high and the company is interested in pushing it higher. The workers are valued because they are important and highly trained.
5. It is about company development because the workers and management will make an improving developing company.
6. The main market is the workers although other markets are also sought.
7. It is competitive but the competition's centerpiece is not destroying the wage scale.

Midwestern Capitalism needs several things to survive:
1. It needs to maintain its internal market.
2. This market is largely determined by the salary scale. When this salary scale is threatened, immigration should be restricted or foreign products should be restricted until salaries are returned to a satisfactory level.

3. It is vulnerable to parasitic infestation by Plantation Capitalism using the generous Midwestern Capitalism's consumption market to make profits by reducing workers wages either in situ by importing slaves, guest workers, or illegal immigrants or externally sourcing products made with poorly paid labor.
4. It needs a boundary that protects its domestic market, its workers, and its industry.

The American System - American Capitalism

Alexander Hamilton, the first Secretary of the Treasury presented his Report on the Subject of Manufactures on December 5, 1791 during George Washington's first term. He borrowed heavily from Mercantilist thought of his day. He thought it expedient to promote the growth of manufacturing by protecting it with a tariff. This had three objectives in his mind:

1) Protect American industry.
2) Raise revenue to pay for the expenses of government.
3) Use the revenue to directly support industry through subsidies.

He recognized that to be a great power America would need a first rate industrial base. To foster this he proposed to support improvements in infrastructure using part of the revenue obtained by the tariff. Congress initially refused to adopt this plan due to opposition by James Madison and his supporters because of concerns about corruption. Madison and Jefferson rather than using subsidies proposed high tariffs and import restrictions to facilitate the growth of industry.

Tariffs were the largest (approaching 95% at times) source of Federal Revenue until the Federal Income Tax was passed in 1913. For the first 120 years of the republic it was largely financed by taxes on imports averaging about 20%. In 1917 with the need for higher taxes for WWI, the income tax receipts finally exceeded the tariff revenue.

During the economic warfare and actual warfare with England in the period 1807 -1815 the desirability of being self sufficient economically was driven home to the Americans, so the Tariff of 1816 was passed and signed into law by James Madison. (He had learned from experience and was now on the side of a higher tariff). It placed a 25% tariff on cotton and woolen production, 30% on iron, leather, and cabinet ware. A 10% discount was applied to items imported on American ships to facilitate the development of an American merchant marine. This tariff was supported by both North and South in the aftermath of the War of 1812, but subsequently the Southern leaders representing/being plantation capitalists began to take a more Free Trade approach whereas the tariff was popular in the North protecting industry and labor from cheaper British products.

In 1824 Henry Clay began referring to an American System which consisted of three main points:

1. Protect industry. This was principally accomplished by tariffs.
2. Develop physical infrastructure. Internal improvements such as the National Road (Cumberland Road), canals, better port facilities. Abraham Lincoln, a follower of Clay would facilitate the Transcontinental Railroad (Union Pacific Railroad) in 1862.
3. Develop financial infrastructure: Examples would be the First Bank of the United States, Second Bank of the United States, etc.

Henry C. Carey, an American economist and adviser to Abraham Lincoln, in his book a *Harmony of Interests,* raises two additional points of American School economic philosophy:

1. Government support for the development of science and education through a public school system and investments in creative research.
2. Rejection of class struggle, in favor of the "Harmony of Interests" between: owners and workers, farmers and manufacturers, the wealthy class and the working class. See Abraham Lincoln's quote, " Republican's are for both the man and the dollar, but in a pinch choose the man."

The contrast between this American System and the "Free Trade" theory from England were recognized by Carey at the time:

"Two systems are before the world;... One looks to increasing the necessity of commerce; the other to increasing the power to maintain it. One looks to underworking the Hindoo, and sinking the rest of the world to his level; the other to raising the standard of man throughout the world to our level. One looks to pauperism, ignorance, depopulation, and barbarism; the other to increasing wealth, comfort, intelligence, combination of action, and civilization. One looks towards

universal war; the other towards universal peace. One is the English system; the other we may be proud to call the American system, for it is the only one ever devised the tendency of which was that of elevating while equalizing the condition of man throughout the world."
- Henry Carey, *The Harmony of Interests*.

The tariff of 1828 was a high protectionist tariff with a 62% tax on 92% of imported goods. This led to protests from the South and the tariff was reduced in 1832. South Carolina was still unhappy and threatened to disregard the tariff. This led to the Nullification Crisis that was averted after posturing (and the threat of Jackson using force on South Carolina) by a decreased Tariff of 1833 that gradually reduced rates until 1842. In 1842 high tariff rates were reinstated by the Black Tariff. This increased Tariff rates from about 20% to 40 %. As expected, when import prices went up, import volumes went down.

During this period of time the American system was opposed by Presidents Jackson, Van Buren, and Polk for several reasons. They thought that the National Bank was a corrupting influence. They were concerned that the infrastructure projects were governmental overreach and served the interests of the connected rather than the common man. They were concerned that large tariffs favored one section of the country over another.

Henry Clay gave a speech called The American System[1] on February 2,3, and 6, 1832. I quote most of it; all of it makes a good read.

Clay makes several points:

1. The first is that a large tariff had been put in place in 1824 and the years since then had been seven years of steady prosperity. It flat out works. Further, the opponents of the legislation had made a series of predictions and were wrong.

> "And if we descend into particulars, we have the agreeable contemplation of a people out of debt; land slowly rising in value , but in a secure and salutary degree; a ready, though not extravagant market for all the surplus productions of our

industry; innumerable flocks and herds browsing and gamboling on ten thousand hills and plains, covered in rich and verdant grasses; our cities expanded, and whole villages springing up as it were, by enchantment; our exports and imports increased and increasing; our tonnage, foreign and coastwise, swelling and fully occupied; the rivers of our interior animated by the perpetual thunder and lightning of countless steamboats; the currency sound and abundant; the public debt of two wars nearly redeemed; and, to crown all, the public treasury overflowing, embarrassing congress, not to find subjects of taxation, but to select the objects which shall be liberated from the impost. If the term of seven years were to be selected of the greatest prosperity which this people have enjoyed since the establishment of their resent Constitution, it would be exactly that period of seven years which immediately followed the passage of the tariff of 1824.

This transformation of the condition of the country from gloom and distress to brightness and prosperity, has been mainly the work of American legislation, fostering American industry, instead of allowing it to be controlled by foreign legislation, cherishing foreign industry. The foes of the American System, in 1824, with great boldness and confidence, predicted, 1st.The ruin of the public revenue, and the creation of a necessity to resort to direct taxation. The gentleman from South Carolina,(Mr. HAYNE) I believe, thought that the tariff of 1824 would operate a reduction of revenue to the large amount of eight millions of dollars.2d.The destruction of our navigation. 3d. The desolation of commercial cities. And 4th The

> augmentation of the price of objects of consumption, and the further decline in that of the articles of our exports. Every prediction which they made has failed- utterly failed. Instead of ruin of the public revenue, with which they sought to deter us from the adoption of the American System, we are now threatened with its subversion, by the vast amounts of the public revenue produced by that system. Every branch of our navigation has increased. As to the desolation of our cities....the assessed value of NY real estate....rose ...(from 52 million) to 95 million."

2. Later in his speech he shows that commodities are decreasing in price. This he ascribes to competition. This is important because one of the main arguments Free Trade advocates make is that it lowers prices.
However, prices will gradually go down in a closed economy with competition because there is a steady improvement in technique of production caused by domestic production so long as there is adequate competition.

> "I hold in my hand a statement, derived from the most authentic source, showing that the identical description of cotton cloth, which sold, in 1817, at 29 cents per yard, was sold, in 1819, at 21 cents; in 1821, at 19% cents; in 1823, at 17 cents; and in 1825, at 14% cents; in 1827, at 13 cents; in 1829, at 9 cents; in 1830, at 9% cents; and in 1831, at from 10% to 11.

Such is the wonderful effect of protection, competition, and improvement in skill, combined!"

"Brown sugar, during ten years, from 1792 to 1802, with a duty of 1% cents per pound, averaged 14 cents per pound. The same article, during ten years, from 1820 to 1830, with a duty of 3 cents, has averaged only 8 cents per pound. Nails, with a duty of 5 cents per pound, are selling at 6 cents. Window glass, eight by ten, prior to the tariff of 1824, sold at $12 or $13 per hundred feet it now sells for $3.75"

"This brings me to consider what I apprehend to have been the most efficient of all the causes in the reduction of the prices of manufactured articles; and that is, COMPETITION. By competition, the total amount of the supply is increased, and by increase of the supply a competition in the sale ensues, and this enables the consumer to buy at lower rates. Of all human powers operating on the affairs of mankind, none is greater than that of competition. It is action and reaction. It operates between individuals in the same nation, and between different nations. It resembles the meeting of the mountain torrent, grooving, by its precipitous motion, its own channel, and ocean's tide. Unopposed, it sweeps everything before it; but, counterpoised, the waters become calm, safe, and regular. It is like the segments of a circle or an arch; taken separately, each is nothing; but, in their combination, they produce efficiency, symmetry, and perfection. By the American System this vast power has been excited in America, and brought into being to act in cooperation or collision with European industry. Europe acts within itself, and with America; and America acts within itself, and with Europe. The consequence is the reduction of prices in both hemispheres. Nor is it fair to argue, from the reduction of prices in Europe, to her own presumed skill and labor, exclusively. We affect her prices, and she affects ours. This must always be the case, at least in reference to any articles as to which there is not a total nonintercourse; and if our industry, by diminishing the demand for her supplies, should produce a diminution in the price of those supplies, it would be very unfair to ascribe that reduction to her ingenuity, instead of placing it to the credit of our own skill and excited industry. Practical men understand very well this state of the case, whether they do or do not comprehend the causes which produce it. I have in my possession a letter from a respectable merchant, well known to me, in which he says, after complaining of the operation of the tariff of 1828 on the articles to which it applies, some of which he had imported, and that his purchases having been made in England before the passage of that tariff was known, it produced such an effect upon the English market, that the articles could not be resold without loss; he adds: "for really it appears that, when additional duties are laid upon an article, it then becomes lower instead of higher." This could not probably happen where the supply of the foreign article did not exceed_ the home demand, unless upon the supposition of the increased duty having excited or stimulated the measure of the home production.

The great law of price is determined by supply and demand. Whatever affects either, affects the price. If the supply is increased, the demand remaining the same, the price declines; if the demand is increased, the supply remaining the same, the price advances; if both supply and demand are undiminished, the price is stationary, and the price is influenced exactly in proportion to the degree of disturbance to the demand or supply. It is therefore a great error to suppose that an existing or new duty necessarily becomes a component element, to its exact amount, of price. If the proportions of demand and supply are varied by the duty, either in augmenting the supply, or diminishing the demand, or vice versa, price is affected, to the extent of that variation. But the duty never becomes an integral part of the price, except in the instances where the demand and the supply remain, after the duty is imposed, precisely what they were before, or the demand is increased, and the supply remains stationary.

Competition, therefore, wherever existing, whether at home or abroad, is the parent cause of cheapness. If a high duty excites production at home, and the quantity of the domestic article exceeds the amount which had been previously imported, the price will fall. This accounts for an extraordinary fact stated by a senator from Missouri. Three cents were laid as a duty upon a pound of lead, by the act of 1828. The price at Galena and the other lead mines afterwards fell to one and a half cents per pound. Now it is obvious that the duty did not, in this case, enter into the price: for it was twice the amount of the price. What produced the fall? It was stimulated production at home, exerted by the temptation of the exclusive possession of the home market. This state of things could not last. Men would not continue an unprofitable pursuit; some abandoned the business, or the total quantity produced was diminished, and living prices have been the consequence. But, break down the domestic supply; place us again in a state of dependence on the foreign source; and can it be doubted that we should, ultimately, have to supply ourselves at dearer rates? It is not fair to credit the foreign market with the depression of prices, produced there by the influence of our competition...."

3. What you can control is your domestic market. Having a vibrant domestic market is vital to the growth of the country.

"I have now to consider the remaining of the two propositions which I have already announced. That is,

2dly. That, under the operation of the American system, the products of our agriculture command a higher price than they would do without it, by the creation of a home market; and, by the augmentation of wealth produced by manufacturing industry, which enlarges our powers of consumption, both of domestic and foreign articles. The importance of the home market is among the established maxims which are universally recognised by all writers and all men. However some may differ as to the relative advantages of the foreign and the home market, none deny to the latter great value and high consideration. It is nearer to us, beyond the control of foreign legislation, and undisturbed by those vicissitudes to which all international intercourse is more or less exposed.

The most stupid are sensible of the benefit of a residence in the vicinity of a large manufactory, or a market town, of a good road, or of a navigable stream, which connects their farms with some great capital. If the pursuits of all men were perfectly the same, although they would be in possession of the greatest abundance of the particular produce of their industry, they might, at the same time, be in extreme want of other necessary articles of human subsistence. The uniformity of the general occupation would preclude all exchanges-all commerce. It is only in the diversity of the vocations of the members of a community that the means can be found for those salutary exchanges which conduce to the general prosperity; and the greater that diversity, the more extensive and the more animating is the circle of exchange. Even if foreign markets were freely and widely open to the reception of our agricultural produce, from its bulky nature, and the distance of the interior, and the dangers of the ocean, large portions of it could never profitably reach the foreign market. But let us quit this field of theory, clear as it is, and look at the practical operation of the system of protection, beginning with the most valuable staple of our agriculture.

In considering this staple, the first circumstance that excites our surprise is the rapidity with which the amount of it has annually increased. Does not this fact, howeyer, demonstrate that the cultivation of it could not have been so very unprofitable? If the business were [ruinous, would more and more have annually engaged in it? The quantity in 1816 was 81 millions of pounds; in 1826, 204 millions; and, in 1830, near 300 millions! The ground of greatest surprise is, that it has been able to sustain even its present price with such an enormous augmentation of quantity. It could not have done it but for the combined operation of three causes, by which the consumption of cotton fabrics has been greatly extended, in consequence of their reduced prices: 1st, competition; 2d, the improvement of labor-saving machinery; and 3dly, the low price of the raw material. The crop of .1819, amounting to 88 millions of pounds, produced $21 millions; the crop of 1823, when the amount was swelled to 174 millions, (almost double that of 1819) produced a less sum, by more than half a million of dollars; and the crop of 1824, amounting to 30 millions of pounds less than that of the preceding year, produced $1.5 million more.

If there be any foundation for the established law of pl}ce, supply, and demand, ought not the fact of this great increase of the supply to account, satisfactorily, for the alleged low price of cotton? Is it necessary to look beyond that single fact to the tariff-to the diminished produce of the mines furnishing the precious metals, or to any other cause, for the solution? This subject is well understood in the South; and, although I cannot approve the practice which has been introduced, of quoting authority, and still less the authority of newspapers, for favorite theories, I· must ask permission of the Senate to read an article from a southern newspaper. [Here Mr. HAYNE requested Mr. CLAY to give the name of the authority, that it might appear whether it was not some other than a southern paper expressing southern sentiments. Mr. CLAY stated that it was from the Charleston City Gazette, one, he believed, of the oldest and most respectable prints in that city, although he was not sure what might be its sentiments on the question which at present divides the people of South Carolina.] The article comprises a full explanation of the low price of cotton, and assigns to it its true cause-increased production.

[Mr. C. read the article as follows:]

From the Charleston City Gazette, copied into the New Orleans

Emporium, January 4.

1st. The greatest fluctuation in the price of cotton was before the tariff of 1824.

2d. Cotton, like every other article of merchandise, has its fixed price, not in America, but in the market of the world, and depends upon the proportion between demand and supply, just as com, which, when it is scarce, sells high, and whei:l plenty sells low.

To illustrate how perfectly the price depends on the demand, it is stated that the crop of 1819, amounting to eighty-eight millions of pounds, sold for twenty-one millions of dollars; while the crop of 1823, amounting to one hundred and seventy millions of pounds, was sold for only twenty millions of dollars! And this before the light tariff of 1824. The cause of this difference in the price of cotton is found in the state of the markets, which were hungry in 1819, and had not a great supply, but were overfed in 1823, and could hardly digest the crop of that year.

The price of cotton fluctuated before the present tariff: and, if the same causes of fluctuation exist, they will produce the same effects, independent of the tariff. It is true cotton has come to be sold at ten cents per pound, that used to bring twenty cents. In this reduction of his profits, the cotton planter only shares the same with the wheat grower. Flour is sold at five dollars per barrel, which formerly brought eight and ten dollars; and the products of the earth generally are low, because they are very abundant.

With respect to cotton, this is to be said further. No mode of investing money in agricultural pursuits, this side of the sugar plantations, has afforded so great an income as the culture of cotton. So that has happened to the cotton planter, which happens to all, viz. a diminution of his income, from the multitudes of those who adopted his lucrative business.

To seek relief from this depressed price of cotton, by repealing the tariff law, is a most inconsiderate step: for the tariff not only creates a new market for raw cotton, but it also converts some of the finest country for growing cotton into sugar plantations. The tariff, by protecting domestic sugars, enables the Louisianian to raise sugar. Remove the tariff from sugars, and the Louisianian cannot compete with the West Indian. Cotton he can raise to better advantage than the Carolinian. So the relief of the cotton planter, sought by the repeal of the protecting tariff, would multiply cotton growers, and cut off the Northeastern market atone and the same blow. What a stroke of nullifying policy that would be!

The price of any thing in market is governed by the supply in market; if that is great, the price is low; if small, the price is high. Whatever has a tendency to consume the stock, increases the price; and whatever has a tendency to increase the stock, diminishes the price of that article in the market.

The terrible manufactures at the North do not add to the stock of cotton; they diminish the stock, and raise the price in the market of the world. They consume vast quantities of cotton, and clear the market of what might otherwise become a drug. A repeal of the tariff law would wind up the Northern factories. When these cease to be consumers, the price of cotton must fall lower than it now is.

Let us suppose that the home demand for cotton, which has been created by the American System, were to cease, and that the 200,000 14 bales, that the home market now absorbs, were thrown into the glutted markets of foreign countries, would not the effect inevitably be to produce a further and great reduction in the price of the article? If there be any truth in the facts and principles which I have before stated, and endeavored to illustrate, it cannot be doubted that the existence of American manufactures has tended to increase the demand, and extend the consumption of the raw material; and that, but for this increased demand, the price of the article would have fallen, possibly one-half, lower than it now is. The error of the opposite argument is, in assuming one thing, which, being denied, the whole fails; that is, it assumes that the whole labor of the United States would be profitably employed, without manufactures. Now, the truth is, that the system excites and creates labor, and this labor creates wealth, and this new wealth communicates additional ability to consume, which acts on all the objects contributing to human comfort and enjoyment. The amount of cotton imported into the two ports of Boston and Providence alone, (during the last year, and it was imported exclusively for the home manufacture) was 109,517 bales.

On passing from that article to others of our agricultural productions, we shall find not less gratifying facts. The total quantity of flour imported into Boston during the same year was 284,504 barrels and 3,955 half barrels; of which, there were from Virginia, Georgetown, and Alexandria, 114,222 barrels; of Indian corn,

581,131 bushels; of oats, 239,809 bushels; of rye, about 50,000 bushels; and of shorts, 33,489 bushels. Into the port of Providence, 71,369 barrels of flour, 216,662 bushels of Indian corn, and 7,772 bushels of rye. And there were discharged at the port of Philadelphia 420,353 bushels of Indian corn, 201,878 bushels of · wheat, and 110,557 bushels of rye and barley. There were slaughtered in Boston during the same year, 1831 (the only northern city from which I have obtained returns), 33,922 beef cattle, 15,400 stores, 84,453 sheep, and 26,871 swine. It is confidently believed that there is not a less quantity of southern flour consumed at the North than 800,000 barrels-a greater amount, probably, than is shipped to all the foreign markets in the world together."

4. There is no real Free Trade. You can lower your tariffs but that does not guarantee that you will have fair access to other markets.

"What would be the condition of the farming country of the United States-of that portion which lies north, east, and west of James River, including a large part of North Carolina, if a home market did not exist for this immense amount of agricultural produce? Without that market, where could it be sold? In foreign markets? If their restrictive laws did not exist, their capacity would not enable them to purchase and consume this vast addition to their present supplies, which must be thrown in, or· thrown away, but for the home market. But their laws exclude us from their markets. I shall content myself by calling the attention of the Senate to Great Britain only. The duties, in the ports of the United Kingdom, on bread stuffs, are prohibitory, except in times of dearth. On rice, the duty is fifteen shillings sterling per hundred weight, being more than 100 percent. On manufactured tobacco, it is nine shillings sterling per pound, or about 2,000 percent. On leaf tobacco, three shillings per pound, or 1,200 percent. On lumber and some other articles, they are from 400 to 1,500 percent more than on similar articles imported from British colonies. In the British West Indies, the duty on beef, pork, hams, and bacon, is twelve shillings sterling per hundred, more than 100 percent on the first cost of beef and pork in the western states. And yet Great Britain is the power in whose behalf we are called upon to legislate', so that we may enable her to purchase our cotton! Great Britain, that thinks only of herself in her own legislation! When have we experienced justice, much less favor, at her hands? When did she shape her legislation in reference to the interests of any foreign powers? She is a great, opulent, and powerful nation; but haughty, arrogant, and supercilious. Not more separated from the rest of the world by the sea that girts her island, than she is separated in feeling, sympathy, or friendly consideration of their welfare. Gentlemen, in supposing it impracticable that we should successfully compete with her in manufactures, do injustice to the skill and enterprise of their own country. Gallant as Great Britain undoubtedly is, we have gloriously contended with her, man to man, gun to gun, ship to ship, fleet to fleet, and army to army. And I have no doubt we are destined to achieve equal success in the more useful, if not nobler contest, for superiority in the arts of civil life.

I could extend and dwell on the long list of articles-the hemp, iron, lead, coal, and other items, for which a demand is created in the home market, by the operation of the American System; but I should exhaust the patience of the Senate. Where, where, should we find a market for all these articles, if it did not exist at home? What would be the condition of the largest portion of our people and of the territory, if this home market were annihilated?

How could they be supplied with objects of prime necessity? What would not be the certain and inevitable decline in the price of all these articles, but for the home market? And allow me, Mr. President, to say, that, of all the agricultural parts of the United States which are benefited by the operation of this system, none are equally so with those which border the Chesapeake Bay, the lower parts of North Carolina, Virginia, and the two shores of Maryland. Their facilities of transportation and proximity to the North give them decided advantages.

5. Keeping the population employed with good paying jobs is every bit as important as low prices.

> But if all this reasoning were totally fallacious-
> if the price of manufactured articles
> were really higher under the American System,
> than without it, I should still argue that high or
> low prices were themselves relative-relative to
> the ability to pay them. It is in vain to tempt,
> to tantalize us with the lower prices of European
> fabrics than our own, if we have nothing
> wherewith to purchase them. If, by the home
> exchanges, we can be supplied with necessary,
> even if they are dearer and worse, articles of
> American production than the foreign, it is
> better than not to be supplied at all. And how
> would the large portion of our country which I
> have described, be supplied, but for the home
> exchanges? A poor people destitute of wealth or
> of exchangeable commodities, has nothing to
> purchase foreign fabrics. To them they are
> equally beyond their reach, whether their cost
> be a dollar or a guinea. It is in this view of the
> matter that Great Britain, by her vast wealthher
> exerted and protected industry-is enabled to
> bear a burden of taxation which, when compared
> to that of other nations, appears enormous;
> but which, when her immense riches are
> compared to theirs, is light and trivial. The gentleman
> from South Carolina has drawn a lively
> and flattering picture of our coasts, bays, rivers,
> and harbors; and he argues that these proclaimed

the design of Providence that we should be a commercial people. I agree with him. We differ only as to the means. He would cherish the foreign, and neglect the internal trade. I would foster both. What is navigation without ships, or ships without cargoes? By penetrating the bosoms of our mountains, and extracting from them their precious treasures; by cultivating the earth, and securing a home market for its rich and abundant products; by employing the water power with which we are blessed; by stimulating and protecting our native industry, in all its forms; we shall but nourish and promote the prosperity of commerce, foreign and domestic."

6. Having a strong industrial base is vital to national security especially in times of war.

"I have hitherto considered the question in reference only to a state of peace; but a season of war ought not to be entirely overlooked. We have enjoyed near twenty years of peace; but who can tell when the storm of war shall again break forth? Have we forgotten, so soon, the privations to which not merely our brave soldiers and our gallant tars were subjected, but the whole community, during the last war, for the want of absolute necessaries? To what an enormous price they rose? And how inadequate the supply was, at any price? The statesman, who justly elevates his views, will look behind as well as forward, and at the existing state of things; and he will graduate the policy which he recommends, to all the probable exigencies which may arise in the republic. Taking this comprehensive range, it would be easy to show that the higher prices of peace, if prices were higher in peace, were more than compensated by the lower prices of war, during which supplies of all essential articles are indispensable to its vigorous, effectual, and glorious prosecution. I conclude this part of the argument with the hope that my humble exertions have not been altogether unsuccessful in showing-

1. That the policy which we have been considering ought to continue to be regarded as the genuine American System.
2. That the free trade system, which is proposed as its substitute, ought really to be considered as the British colonial system.
3. That the American System is beneficial to all parts of the Union, and absolutely necessary to much the larger portion.
4. That the price of the great staple of cotton, and of all our chief productions of agriculture, has been sustained and upheld, and a decline averted by the protective system.
5. That, if the foreign demand for cotton has been at all diminished by the operation of that system, the diminution has been more than compensated in the additional demand created at home.
6. That the constant tendency of the system,

by creating competition among ourselves, and between American and European industry, reciprocally acting upon each other, is to reduce prices of manufactured objects.

7. That, in point of fact, objects within the scope of the policy of protection have greatly fallen in price.

8. That if, in a season of peace, these benefits are experienced in a season of war, when the foreign supply might be cut off, they would be much more extensively felt.

9. And, finally, that the substitution of the British colonial system for the American System, without benefiting any section of the Union, by subjecting us to a foreign legislation, regulated by foreign interests, would lead to the prostration of our manufactures, general impoverishment, and ultimate ruin."

<u>With the election of Lincoln in 1860, the opposition of the Plantation Capitalists disappeared politically and the American System was enacted with a tripling</u>

of the tariff, construction of the transcontinental railroad, and the passage of the Legal Tender Act (February 25, 1862). Except for a return to the gold standard, this was the American economic system until the Wilson Administration. It was also the policy of the United States in the Roaring Twenties. During this time America grew to be the dominant economic power on the planet.

Several notes on the American System of Capitalism:

1) It is about national development. Rather than comparative advantage where different countries specialize in various products, the American System will tend to make each country of a certain size self sufficient.
2) It is about development of a domestic market for goods by paying workers a living wage. The primary market is domestic.
It is open to foreign trade on a limited basis. Thank you for the revenue.
3) It is about domestic competition. In the early 19th century monopolies were not established. Later during the Theodore Roosevelt administration, due to concentration of industry President Roosevelt initiated antitrust enforcement against Standard Oil.
4) It has worked before and was abandoned after WWII not because it had been proven inferior to Free Trade with respect to the average American citizen but as an underpinning to the establishment of an American trading empire and to serve the political ends of the Cold War.
5) Note that in 1832 the United States had almost paid off the public debt of the Revolutionary War, the Louisiana Purchase, and the War of 1812. As a mark of comparison after 40 years of globalization our present debt of 18 trillion is an underwhelming performance.

Rhenish Capitalism.

Another form of capitalism to be considered is Rhenish capitalism which is of the family of trust based capitalisms. Rhenish refers to the Rhine river and encompasses the Netherlands, Belgium, Luxembourg, Switzerland, and of course Germany. Germany grew at a rate of 8.2% per year in the 1950's, at a rate of 4.4% from 1960 to 1973, and at a rate of 2.2% from 1973-1980 and 1.9% per year from 1980-1990. German and Swiss companies continue to compete at a high level in spite of having a relatively high wage scale (BMW, Siemens, Roche). There are four distinguishing features of the German model:

1. There is a higher level of cooperation between businesses and corporations than is seen in American or British firms.
2. West German banks have played a larger role in the development of German industry than seen in the US or Britain.
3. The German state has been less free trade oriented and has served to protect and nurture German firms more than has been the case with American or British firms.
4. Organized labor and industry have had a far more cooperative relationship in Germany than in America or England.[3]

1. There is a higher level of cooperation between businesses and corporations than is seen in American or British firms.

German industry has historically shown greater cooperation between different business entities than in the US. In this way it more parallels the Japanese or Korean examples of a keiretsu than the American model. The toleration of a cartel has been greater in these countries than historically was the case in the US. Also in Germany there has been a more paternalistic attitude of the corporation to the needs of the employees (again more paralleling the Japanese model). German industry has been more concentrated in producer goods than consumer goods vis a vis the US.[4]

2. West German banks have played a larger role in the development of German industry than seen in the US or Britain.

German banks have been central to the development of German industry.

German banks hold and control shares in German companies. They sit on the boards and serve as a long term loyal sources of capital and consultation. They know the companies they finance and the competitive pressures they face. They are long term backers of German industry .[5]

German banks have historically provided much of the capital for German industry and they sit on the boards and monitor the companies they have loaned money to. When necessary they will initiate management changes and restructuring. Thus German corporate governance has had much more potent feedback in the boardroom. The CEO has to answer to his loan officer on an ongoing basis in contradistinction to the American Board which the CEO typically fills with compliant individuals who will not obstruct him. This no doubt has helped keep unwarranted bonuses and stock options more in check in German firms when compared to American firms and serves as an independent interested voice in long term management. This also allows the banks to make more informed decisions with respect to capital allocation than typically occurs on Wall Street where your typical (non insider connected) investor has nowhere near the level of information than the German bank will have about the company it loaned money too. Not only the does the bank have inside information on the firm we are discussing (firm A), they will have good information on other firms they have loaned money too (firms B, C, D,....). This makes them better investors as well. It is no doubt connected to our first point of the higher level of cooperation between firms and a tendency not to be as vigilant at breaking up cartels. (Obviously this has pluses and minuses).

3. The German state has been less free trade oriented and has served to protect and nurture German firms more than has been the case with American or British firms.

Friedrich List was a German American economist (1789-1846). He immigrated to Pennsylvania in 1825 and absorbed ideas from Hamilton's work and Henry Clay's American system. List advocated a theory of "national economics". He pointed out that actions an individual may make may be personally beneficial but poor for society. "Slavery may be a public calamity for a country, nevertheless some people may do very well in carrying on the slave trade and in holding slaves." List noted that Napoleon's "Continental System" which had had the objective of restricting British trade had been good for the development of German industry. "I perceived that the popular(Smith's Free Trade) theory took no account of nations, but simply of the entire human race on one hand, or the single individual on the other. I saw clearly that free competition between two nations which are highly civilized can be mutually beneficial in case both of them are in a nearly equal position of industrial development, and that any nation which owing to misfortunes is behind others in industry, commerce, and navigation ....must first of all strengthen her own individual powers, in order to fit herself to enter into free competition with more advanced nations. In a word, I perceived the distinction between cosmopolitan and political economy."

List considered Britain's advocation of Free Trade self seeking and said,

" Any nation which by means of protective duties and restrictions on navigation has raised her manufacturing power and her navigation to such a degree of development that no other nation can sustain free competition with her, can do nothing wiser than to throw away these ladders of her greatness, to preach to other nations the benefits of free trade, and to declare in penitent tones that she has hitherto wandered in the paths of error, and now has for the first time succeeded in discovering the truth."

List's plan for German growth included a customs union for German lands, protection for German industry, and a German marine with a Navigation act.

This plan was executed by Otto von Bismarck who picked up the ladders of greatness. This led to the emergence of Germany as a great power in the later half of the 19th century. Similar measures have been taken by the Japanese following WWII and Chinese recently.

The German state has not completely left this successful model and continues to nurture her industries. The German tools for development include tariff protection, underwriting banks, encouraging long term investor relations, and subsidizing strategic sectors of industry.[6]

4. Organized labor and industry have had a far more cooperative relationship in Germany than in America or England.

There is a strong system of vocational training. There is a high level of technical skill. The empowered workers take higher level of responsibility and pride in the companies. This leads to more cooperative higher performing business organizations.[7] There is in German capitalism a stronger "stakeholder" ethos in business management.

Several notes on this model of capitalism.

1) It is about community development. It is about growing strong businesses and strong well trained work forces.

2) It is protectionist.

3) The toleration of cartels is a point of distinction from the later stages of the American System when Theodore Roosevelt used antitrust laws to break up Standard Oil.

4) The strong organized labor presence should help to some extent to head off the effects of Plantation Capitalism, where the business owner tries to make his margin by breaking the wage scale of his workers.

5) Without strong protection laws, this system will ultimately be vulnerable to Plantation Capitalism. Judging by the levels of Turkish guest worker immigration levels, and other calamities in Europe, it will take good leadership to maintain an environment where this form of high trust capitalism can continue to flourish.

6) When functioning properly, the banking system supports local industry and the local economy, rather than loaning money around the world to people scarcely know.

1) Richard Hofstader, The American Political Tradition, Vintage Books, 1948. p120

2) Henry Clay, In Defense of The American System, February 2,3, and 6, 1832. Archived in Classic Senate Speeches.

3) David Coates, Models of Capitalism, Polity Press, 2000. p 66- 72.

4) Ibid., p 66-67.

5) Ibid., p 67.

6) Ibid., p 68 - 69.

7) Ibid., p 69 -72.

Mathematical Modeling

"For professional economists, after Malthus, were apparently unmoved by the lack of correspondence between the results of their theory and the facts of observation; -a discrepancy which the ordinary man has not failed to observe, with the result of his growing unwillingness to accord to economists that measure of respect which he gives to other groups of scientists whose theoretical results are confirmed by observation when they are applied to the facts."

- John Maynard Keynes
The General Theory of Employment, Interest, and Money. Chapter III . 1935.

The trade deficit and budget deficit are roughly correlated. This is of course no accident. John Maynard Keynes was the preeminent economist of the twentieth century and he developed a mathematical description of the economic problem of his day - The Great Depression. His description neglected foreign trade to simplify the discussion. However, since foreign trade is central to the ideas in this essay, we can easily expand his model to account for trade. By reworking Keynes basic equations to account for foreign trade, we can get an economic model that predicts what is actually going on.

Keynes fundamental equation that demand for labor P(N) = the production of N workers = D (total demand)=D1 (consumption of N workers demand) + D2 (investment demand) or

P(N) = D1 + D2; alternatively
(value produced by N workers)
= (consumption by N workers) + (investment demand)
= Production (of N workers already hired).

According to Keynes, a modest increase in the amount of investment demand D2 will cause an increase in the number of workers and an increase in consumption demand. An increase in government spending will have a multiplier effect. If the multiplier is 3, increasing the demand for workers by 100,000 through government spending, which we will label G, will result in 300,000 people getting jobs, not just the 100,000 who were directly hired.

Or, Production (workers already hired) + Production of workers hired directly by government spending + Production of workers who were hired as secondary effect of government spending =
= D1(N) + D2(investment demand) + Demand caused by the consumption of the workers who were hired by the government spending + Demand of workers hired as a secondary effect of government spending
= D1 (N) + D2(N) + G + G x (multiplier -1)
= D1 (N) + D2(Investment demand) + G x multiplier.

Or, to substitute the numbers above:
P(N) + P(100,000 direct hires) + P(200,000 indirect hires)
= D1(N) + D2 + G x multiplier.

This is Keynes basic model used to describe a large economy with negligible foreign trade. This was used to model the world of the Great Depression (Keynes' world). Keynes gave a hand waving and little quoted argument in favor of mercantilist theory but did not flesh it out with equations. This is easy and straight forward to do.

Lets simply modify the equation to account a trade surplus.
Demand for the production of the workers in society then equals (the workers consumption) + (new investment) + (trade surplus) x the multiplier.
or
P(N) = D1+ D2 + S (trade surplus) x the multiplier.

Thus China has effective demand based on D1(what Chinese workers consume) + D2 (what investments are made in China) + S (China's trade surplus) x the multiplier.
The trade surplus is mathematically indistinguishable from investment demand or government spending and has a multiplier effect. If the multiplier is 4 in China, 4 million Chinese working to produce textiles and furniture for the US will cause additional demand in China to hire an additional 12 million Chinese to service the needs and wants of the 4 million whose jobs are a direct result of the surplus.

In an unfortunate country running a trade deficit, S is a negative number. The multiplier is the same (for small perturbations). If the multiplier is 4 in the United States, the loss of 1,000,000 textile jobs from imports will result in the loss of 3,000,000 additional jobs as the textile workers no longer have money to buy cars, furniture, new houses, etc. The results of this trade deficit are so devastating that the government responds by massive deficit spending after a delay. Keynes equation can be restated:
P(N) = D1 + D2 + S(trade surplus) x multiplier + G (government deficit spending) x multiplier + M (private sector deficit spending) x multiplier.

Our theory predicts that a rising trade deficit will cause unemployment, or increased government spending or both. Lets look at the historical data.

Growth in U.S. National Debt vs. Cumulative Trade Deficit, 1976-2012 (see note 4)

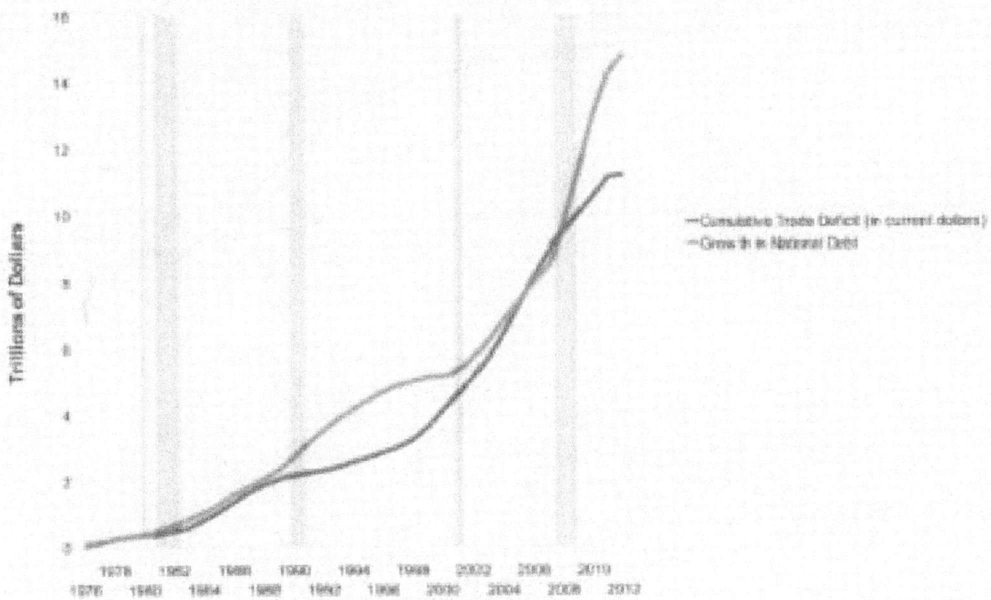

Notes:
1. Cumulative trade deficit expressed in current dollars.
2. Sources: U.S. Treasury (national debt); Bureau of Economic Analysis (trade deficit)
3. U.S. National debt was $0.53 trillion in 1975. Chart above shows growth in the debt from that point, not the actual debt.
4. 2012 data through January.
5. Recessions shown in yellow bars.

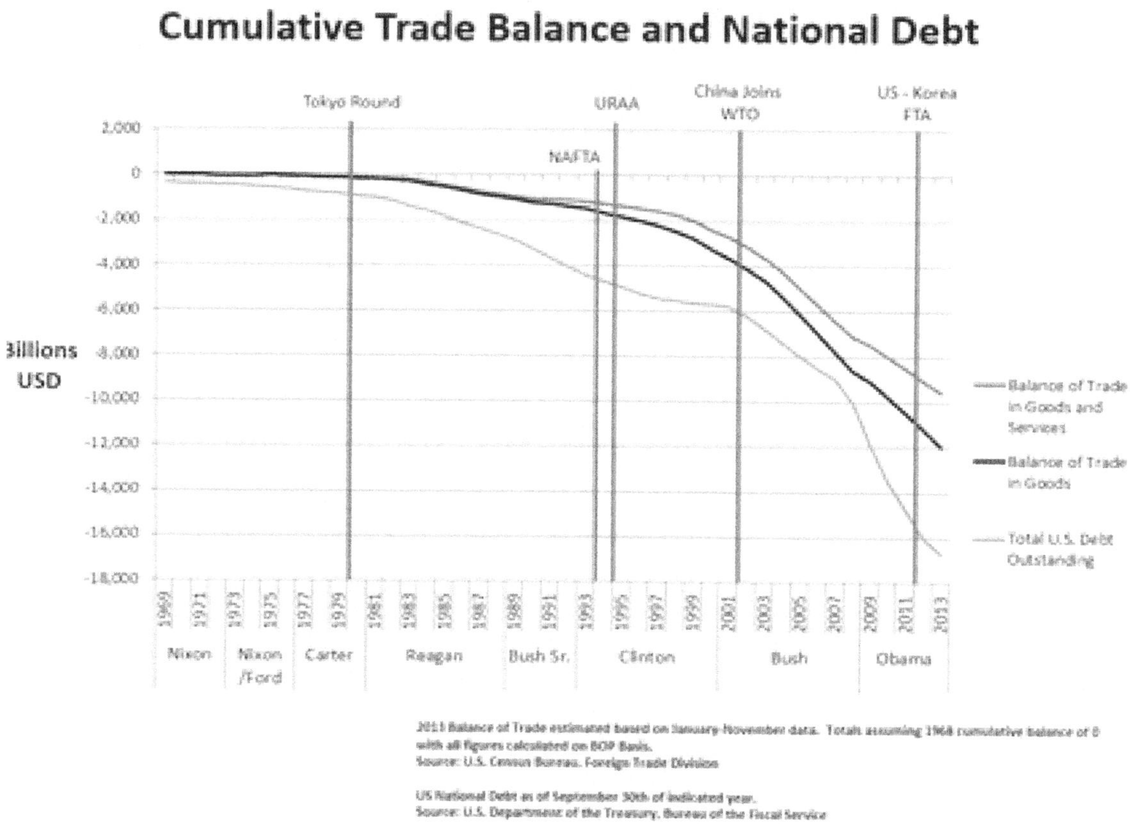

As the above graphical representation shows, the cumulative trade deficit and the budget deficit are strongly linked in direction and order of magnitude. This is a verification of our theory. In order to control the internal state of our economy, controlling trade flows is necessary. <u>There is an accounting identity that net national savings equals the trade surplus.</u>

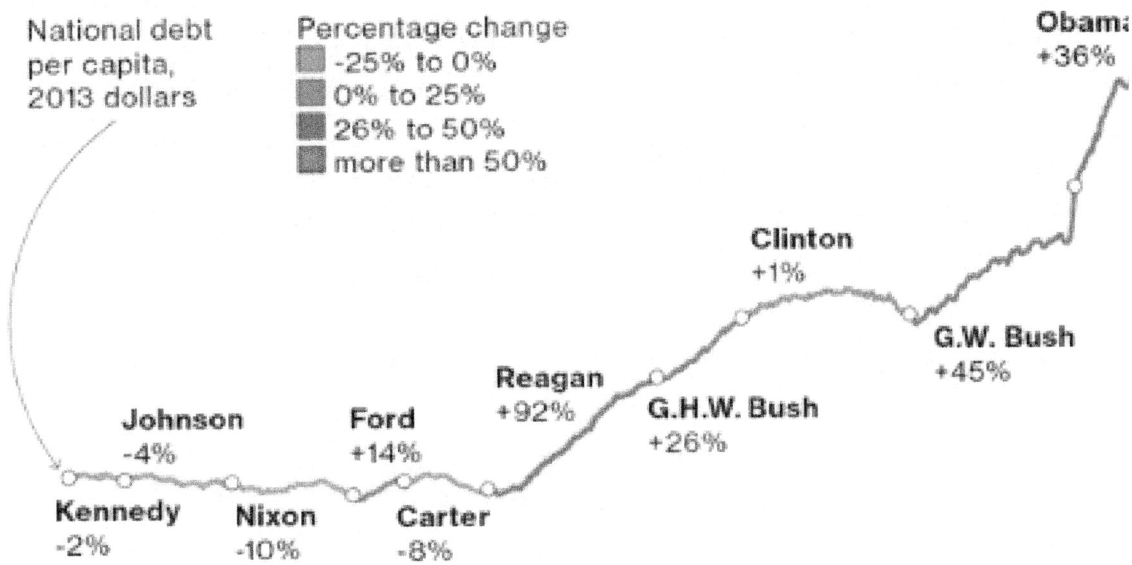

GRAPHIC BY BLOOMBERG BUSINESSWEEK, DATA: U.S. TREASURY, COMPILED B

At the time of this writing the national debt is about 56,000 dollars per person or 140,000 dollars per taxpayer.
The median net worth of an American family decreased from 73,874 to 68,828 between 2000 and 2011. The national debt increased from 5.6 trillion on 6/1/2000 to 14.3 trillion on 6/1/2011. This is an increase of 8.7 trillion dollars.
If the median American family had to pay their share of the national debt they would have a negative net worth. Observation tells us that the trend is not favorable.

To maintain the same level of employment with a trade deficit, either governmental deficit spending or private sector deficit spending needs to replace the lost demand caused by the trade deficit. Americans have tried both with devastating results for the middle class and the government balance sheets. The extraordinary low interest rates we are experiencing are designed to increase borrowing and stimulate the economy. The mortgage bubble was the result of private sector deficit spending (M) and it was not sustainable for long. This debt is now to some extent being nationalized with the Federal Reserve buying mortgage backed securities. The Bush and Obama administrations have tried to stimulate the economy with deficit spending. Without this stimulation the economy would go into deflationary collapse as the trade deficit sucked the jobs away. As we are now, there is pain in society with 23 million unemployed, but the stimulation is preventing social upheaval. Of late there has been more stimulation than deficit so it is possible we will have a short term recovery. One can see mathematically that the amount of deficit spending (chiefly governmental) must roughly equal the trade deficit to maintain the same level of employment.

This is like heating the house with the doors and windows open. Perversely, this transfers power to Washington and to the financial centers in New York. Our government needs to print the money we send overseas. Those close to the government furnace in finance, healthcare, or education are relatively well off. If you are in textiles, plastics, and furniture you feel the glacier. This is like an alcoholic who has burnt all his fuel oil and his firewood trying to keep the house warm with the windows open, and who now wants to burn grandma's dining room table but still refuses to shut the window. This is a boundary problem, and just as a heated house must close its doors, and a cell needs to maintain its cell membrane, a modern economy must be able to control its trade policy if it is to protect its workers and economy from destabilizing competition.

This misallocation of financial power from the country at large to the central government is leading to an increasingly top down economy. This politicalization of the economy opens the door towards a more bureaucratic society where business becomes an inside game of meeting the government's demands rather than the real needs of the society at large. This can lead to inefficiencies, investments that serve artificial needs , and bridges to nowhere. The paperwork in education and health care are growing rapidly without a corresponding improvement in care. More powerful larger entities write the legislation to favor them at the expense of smaller businesses with less resources to lobby Congress and the White House. This leads to an economy more based on patronage than performance which in the long term is not healthy and will lead to decreased competitiveness.

Discussion of D2, private investment.

A brief summary of Keynes observations follows:

According to Keynes, there is a number called the marginal efficiency of capital. This is the interest rate at which you just barely break even buying a piece of capital equipment entirely financed with borrowed money. Keynes says that in aggregate, if entrepreneurs can make money by borrowing money, and investing in equipment, and hiring people they will do it. If the interest rate is too high for them to make money doing this, they will not invest and demand will drop. For society, he hypothesizes, there is an aggregate marginal efficiency of capital, and if the interest rate is above this, the economy will contract, and if it is below this the economy will expand.

Keynes says a rational investor makes the following calculation. Say you are buying a sawmill priced at 1million dollars and you have a firm expectation that it will yield 250,000 for the first 8 years. Keynes would say that the sawmill has a value of a 250,000 dollar zero interest bond with a 1 year maturity + a 250,000 dollar bond with a two year maturity + additional bonds with 3, 4, 5, 6, 7, 8 year maturities.

Let's calculate the value of these hypothetical annuities at a hypothetical 10% interest rate:
The (value of the first year annuity) x our yearly yield at 10% = (value of annuity) x 1.1 = 250,000.
or value of annuity = 250000 / 1.1 = 227,272.
The value of the second year return would be 250,000/ (1.1 x 1.1) = 206611.
The value of the third year of return would be further discounted by dividing by 1.1 again to yield 187829.

The fourth year would yield 170753.
The fifth year would yield 155230.
The sixth year would yield 141118.
The seventh year would yield 128289.
The eighth year would yield 116626.

Keynes hypothetical investor would sum these terms to get 1,333,728. This is greater than 1,000,000 so a rational man would invest. The marginal efficiency of capital in this investment is greater than 10%.

If the return was 187444 per year x 8 years, the discounted value of the investment is 1,000,000 dollars, so the marginal efficiency of capital would be 10 %. Our investor would probably sit on the sidelines, but he might reconsider the deal of interest rates dropped.

If the return is less than 187,444 per year our investor would actually lose money on the deal, so it would be an absolute nonstarter at 10 % interest rates.

This is better information than most investors actually have. Anticipating business conditions 8 years hence is an inherently inaccurate endeavor. Prudent entrepreneurs would want a margin of safety and would not invest at the limit of their margin of safety. Banks or other sources of capital will want to see the entrepreneur's model and then they should handicap it to get an assurance that they get their money back. Banks will generally want additional collateral. Keynes recognized this and said that in reality most investment decisions are not made on rational complete calculations because in the absence of complete foreknowledge such calculations are not practical; instead the decision to invest and grow is based on "animal spirits". This is true as far as it goes, but this idea can be developed much further. Lets look at our business animal- the entrepreneur.

2. The Future Function.

The Entrepreneur's decision on when and where to invest.

Our protagonist is the entrepreneur who has an idea and wants to bring it to fruition. He will model the idea in his head, and then develop a plan to make it happen. He will model the cash flow and see if the idea makes sense. He will develop a business plan and then try to implement it if he believes it will work.

Typically he will start small in a field he thinks he knows and for which he has a deep passion. He will encounter problems ,and if he is successful, solve them rapidly. After a period of time, he will have a tested working plan with positive cash flow and will be ready to expand.

Note that there has already been a significant Darwinian cull of plans that were hopeless/bad, a cull of plans that were poorly executed, and a cull of entrepreneurs who had to quit because of personal crises or exhaustion. Our more seasoned entrepreneur then begins to forecast the future with something like actual numbers rather than pie in the sky because he has an ongoing business. He has tried things that didn't work and has found things that do work. To be slightly facetious, he uses the Future function F(t) for his future forecast with time as the variable. This function can then be expressed as a Taylor Polynomial[1] where :

F is the future function.

t is time.

t_0 is now.

$$\text{Then } F(t) = F(t_0) + \frac{dF(t_0)}{dt} \times (t - t_0) + \frac{1}{2!}\,\frac{d^2\,F(t_0)}{(dt)^2} \times (t - t_0)^2$$

$$+ \quad + \frac{1}{3!} \frac{d^3F(t_0)}{(dt)^3} \times (t - t_o)^3 + \ldots$$

$F(t_0)$ is where the business is right now. This is roughly represented by the balance sheet.

$\frac{dF(t_o)}{dt}$ is the change in the business right now. It is roughly represented by the cash flow or income statement.

$\frac{d^2F(t_0)}{(dt)^2}$ is the anticipated change in the income - i.e. the growth rate of income.

This is less concrete than the first two terms but necessary for intermediate forecasting. A good entrepreneur must have a good feel for this.

$\frac{d^3F(t_0)}{(dt)^3}$ is the change in the rate of growth.

This is difficult to anticipate with accuracy but a qualitative feel for this is necessary for business planning.

Defining terms in this way allows several observations:
1. $F(t_0)$ (Balance Sheet) (Book Value)

Businesses that are going to make investments and hire people have usually made money in the past as evidenced by their balance sheets. The three principal sources of capital to invest are (1) money already on the balance sheet, (2) loans, and (3)new investors. Money already on the balance sheet is typically from running a successful business. (There are a few companies that previously raised money for an idea and grew from allocations of capital from investors based on high hopes rather than actual profits as in the dot com era, but this would not be the way to run a national economy). Loans from prudent bankers are going to use assets from companies which have a pattern of making money for collateral. *So rather than "animal spirits" being the cause of entrepreneurs directing capital for investment, the main driver is a pattern of making money in the past and in the present. In fact, the "animal spirit" for a going concern is connected at the hip to making money.* When profits are high, companies search for ways to put their profits to work. When losses are being incurred, cost containment becomes paramount. Typically, new investors are easier to attract when companies are making money and profits are increasing.

(There are fields such as biotechnology where much of the investment is based on the fantasy of future transformative profits - these stocks tend to be extremely interest rate sensitive as it is far easier to sell these ideas without profits in a boom rather than in a recession).

2. $\frac{dF(t_o)}{dt}$ (Profit)---(How things are going right now)
(Earnings part of price earnings)

Businesses with profits have an inherent plan for growth: Do more of what they are already doing. This allows entrepreneurs to do what they love. Companies with profits have a bias toward growth. Most new hires in an economy will be in companies that are already growing. There is almost always a "jobless recovery " before there is a real recovery. In addition to the obvious business plan above, as outlined in point number one, these same companies will also have access to capital from their balance sheets, lenders, and capital markets. What they need is new markets for an expanded scope. In an expanding economy this can be accomplished by finding new customers. In a stagnant or contracting market, company growth will be through competition.

Businesses with losses, on the other hand have a completely different psychology. Their focus is on reversing the downward trend and conserving cash. There is a need to analyze, listen to customers, listen to employees, make adjustments, and develop a new plan for the future. Until a functional plan is in effect spending will be curtailed.

3. $\frac{d^2F(t_0)}{(dt)^2}$ (Growth of Profit)---(Plans for the future based on predictable issues)

(Is this a growth stock or not?)

Expanding businesses with growing profits in the short run at least are in a position to hire more people and are doing things well. Monitoring opportunities to grow and potential predictable bottlenecks to growth while controlling costs is routine management of a business. Identifying new markets and competitive pressures is an ongoing process. If in management's informed opinion it makes sense to invest and hire people to increase profitability, the company will scale up their operations. If, on the other hand, management senses that hard times lie ahead the company may wish to reduce investment, lower the headcount, reduce the rate of growth, and save cash. A decrease in growth of profitability may signal increasing pressures building that will soon begin to cut into profits. An entrepreneur's evaluation of standard semi predictable business opportunities is what Keynes is describing in his discussion above.

4. $\frac{d^3F(t_0)}{(dt)^3}$ (Change in the growth of profit)---

(Plans for future growth based on unpredictable issues)

Businesses are also buffeted by a variety of forces they can't predict. Many of these forces the entrepreneur may be partly aware of but uncertain as to their effect such as is a competitive drug going to make the drug they are selling obsolete if you are in the pharmaceutical business. Businesses also develop ideas that initially are of uncertain value - they could prove worthless or they could remake the company over time. A business will typically try to develop an idea with as small a commitment of cash as reasonably possible until they get a clear picture of how this idea can be turned into cash-flow, at which time they will scale it up.

Several notes on our model.

1. Predicting the future is accurate as long as its not the future. (When t-t0 is small, the higher order terms can be neglected). When you drive at 60 miles per hour, you can blink your eyes with impunity. The last look you had with your eyes accurately predicts the future for the moment you blink. If, on the other hand, you text your daughter at 60 mph, taking your eyes off the road has significant risks. Probably you will get away with it, but you might hurt yourself or someone else. The longer period of time your eyes are off the road makes the map of the future from your last look less accurate. If due to deep exhaustion, you decide to take a 10 minute nap driving at 60 miles per hour, you will go off roading. You will likely wreck your car, you might, heaven forbid, kill

somebody- maybe yourself. Your last look at the road was 10 miles back and has no bearing on present conditions.

Much of business practice is based on keeping commitments of capital within the predictable easy to visualize future- get paid back in the near future. Several of the Toyota principals are linked to this. Using a pull system of production where things are made based on demand rather batch production and hoping you can sell them is the most obvious. Stabilizing production decreases the need for commitment of capital. Using outside suppliers helps keep the company nimble and able to scale up and scale down production with a minimal commitment of cash. Building a culture that stops to fix problems and gets quality right the first time also will tend to make a company more accountable and flexible. Finally, the Toyota principle of *genchi genbutsu,* go see for yourself where leaders directly interact and visualize their factory / business is helpful in a number of ways one of which is they are predicting the future based on right now, not last year's annual report.

If our entrepreneur can get paid back in the time frame where his model of the future holds, much of the uncertainty of capitalism is eliminated. On the other hand, if he needs to make long term commitments such as a real estate purchase using leverage, the future may be less clear. The commitment of central banks around the world to low inflation is to some extent a method of derisking real estate investment.

2. When your prediction fails, it is failing because the higher order terms in our Taylor Series have supervened. At this point the old model is worthless. You need to open your eyes before proceeding. Fast - you just ran off the road. You are likely at a strategic inflection point.

3. Throughout our model, companies that have made profits, are making profits, and hope to make more profits are the building blocks upon which D2 (investment demand) is based. They will make commitments based on opportunities as they see them with a satisfactory risk / reward ratio with an emphasis on decreasing risk.
Lowering interest rates will increase the general business activity which will help companies make money and make them more likely to increase investment. It will as Keynes outlined, decrease the value of the null investment - buying short term bonds. Lowering interest rates of course works with a time delay - companies need to become profitable before they feel like investing money and hiring people. If the business environment is bad and they are not returned to profitability by the change in interest rates, they are not going to invest in new equipment. Businesses need to see profits or the immediate prospects of profits before they will hire new people in a significant way.

4. Our model says nothing so far about where this new investment will take place.

Let's look at profits briefly since so much of our entrepreneur's actions depend on them.

Profits = Sales - Expenses.
Sales are dependent on the market for a product, the competition within that market, and access to that market. In general, these are less under the entrepreneurs direct control than expenses.

Expenses = Cost of Workers + Cost of Taxes + Cost of Interest + Cost of Land + Cost of Equipment + Cost of Materials + Cost of Utilities + Legal Costs + Market development costs (advertising, brand development, etc) + Product Development Costs + Transportation Costs + Other costs.

The entrepreneur will try to maximize sales while reducing expenses.

Given the same access to a given market, he will seek to lower his labor costs by several methods:
1. Relocating his factory to an area with a cheap labor supply- thus the move in factories from New England, to the American South, to Mexico, and then to China. If the prevailing wage in Mexico is 3 dollars per hour and in the US is 12 dollars per hour this isn't a rocket science decision.
2. Bringing in cheaper labor- thus the need to import workers to work jobs that are more difficult to move such as in healthcare, farming, meatpacking, etc.
3. Colluding with other entrepreneurs to hold wages down. That this actually happens was recently demonstrated in Silicon Valley at Apple and other high tech firms. If it happens at this high end of the market, it undoubtedly happens throughout much of the economy.

4. Outsourcing production or service.
5. Increasing the productivity of labor by improving management, running a tighter ship (reducing waste), and investing in labor saving equipment.

If you live in a developed economy, the first two methods are intellectually easy for the entrepreneur and they will tend to lower the wage scale and employment level. The third method of reducing expenses is slightly more surreptitious but will also tend to hold wages down. Outsourcing production or service is a part of the economic landscape and when used to promote flexibility may increase labor productivity. When the outsourcing is to a low wage jurisdiction for the purposes of lowering the wage scale of the production of the item or service, the overall effect is to lower wages. Note that option number 5 is the hardest for the entrepreneur requiring more thought, energy, and dedication than the other methods - this is the option that will lead to a wealthier society.

Given the same access to a given market, he will seek to lower his tax costs by several methods:
1. Locating his business in a low tax jurisdiction.
2. Negotiating special tax breaks for locating a business in a given jurisdiction (Which state - city can put together the best package for my business?).
3. When a business operates in several jurisdictions with an international supply chain, the entrepreneur will arrange his accounting so his profits are assigned to the lowest tax jurisdiction. An international oil company may have most of its profits in a subsidiary in Panama.
4. Similarly, purchases can be performed through jurisdictions with low / no sales tax.

The entrepreneur will also seek to lower his interest rate and other expenses as much as can reasonably be done. The entrepreneur may decide for quality of life (and personal security) reasons to live in a developed country. He will likely move wealth to perceived safe jurisdictions such as offshore banking with the actual assets in a developed country.

5. Lobbying/corrupting the government to obtain tax breaks for his business.

As briefly outlined above, to increase investment demand in a developed country in a globalized economy, it is necessary for profits to increase but that alone is insufficient. Job creation requires additional incentives. This is especially true if the country is running a trade deficit and a budget deficit which is a quick dashboard assessment that (1) the sovereign is using (what should be) extraordinary means to stimulate the economy, and (2) that the stimulation is causing job creation outside the realm.

Let's examine ways the government can use to motivate the entrepreneur to locate his investment locally. The sovereign could lower the cost of labor. This method is often used when entrepreneurs are the sovereign as in Barbados or the slave states of the American South. It is being used in the developed world today largely because business has corrupted the governments and encouraged open immigration. There are several problems with this approach. The most obvious is that the average salary is decreased causing pain in the country for the average citizen. The second is that the displaced worker in a developed country has a larger chance of becoming a ward of the welfare state increasing expenses to the sovereign. The third is that since the workers are making less money, they can pay less taxes. The fourth is that since the workers have a vague sense they are being sold out, they are less loyal which in time of war could lead to a lower incentive to fight. The fifth reason is that when workers are no longer valued, they internalize this, leading to moral degradation- they are more likely to drink heavily, smoke, and use illicit drugs. The sixth reason is that when workers are no longer valued they are more likely to break the law leading to a higher rate of incarceration -the additional costs in the criminal justice system and prison system are high. The most significant problem is that lowering the wage is decreasing demand since these same workers are to a real extent the market in the country. When you cut their wages you are decreasing their purchases which is decreasing domestic sales - this leads to a general impoverishment of society.

The government can lower taxes. This is tricky, of course. In a recession/ depression this is the fastest most reliable way of immediately increasing profits and reviving the animal spirits of businesses. However, the default fiscal position in peacetime should be a slight budget surplus to build up reserves to be available in time of war or other extraordinary disaster. The tax code is also a primary method by which the government sets incentives to modify behavior. A payroll tax is an obvious disincentive for the entrepreneur to invest locally and hire citizens to work. Income taxes are similar in increasing the cost of domestic labor. Taxes on energy discourage energy consumption and increase transportation costs.

The government could in theory spend less money stabilizing the world. The United States has spent an extraordinary amount of money since WWII to stabilize the world and extend the rule of law. This has increased the security of investing overseas increasing the propensity of entrepreneurs to invest outside the United States. Decreasing piracy, for instance, makes overseas investment security more closely approach the level of security in Utah or Minnesota by de-risking sea transport. Overall, the benefits of a more peaceful secure world for business probably outweigh the costs of disengagement, but they do have a domestic economic cost. Machiavelli writes of empires that are healthy showing their strongest economic growth centrally (Bring it home to Rome!), where as those empires that are in decline show greater economic vitality at the periphery (Do the deal in Damascus). This is a tension in empire through the ages. If the central government attempts to extract revenue or an artificial favorable balance of trade from the periphery, those being protected do not appreciate their protection but only see the costs as in the Americans resenting the British throwing the tea in Boston Harbor and revolting, etc. If, on the other hand, the empire subsidizes the periphery the cost is borne domestically leading to a decline of the empire.

Since World War II, governments have used interest rate modification to stimulate or slow the economy. This works by (1) modifying the entrepreneur's cost of money and (2) stimulating or suppressing domestic demand partly by inducing the population to take on more debt (buy a new house) or pay off debt if the interest rate rises as in the Volcker years.

The costs of land, utilities, equipment, materials are generally set by the market although government regulation and taxation can be quite significant factors influencing these costs. Legal costs are complicated and related to setting the rules of the business game. Pharmaceutical development in the United States which is highly regulated with strong patent protection is quite different than the pharmaceutical business in India with weak patent protection and less regulation. Entrepreneurs will constantly try to have these laws modified to meet their needs which may be quite different from the needs of the public at large. The local rancher may want strong environmental protection, the oil driller may want less environmental oversight. Large banks may want to destroy the Glass Stegall Act, the public may lose if they get what they want.

Improving domestic transportation and communication should in general be stimulative to the economy and investment.

When the above methods have been tried and found to be insufficient to stabilize the balance of trade and lower unemployment to an acceptable level, the sovereign government should try something else.

(They have been tried for 40 years and the result has been 40 years of no raise in the average wage adjusted for inflation. The result has been no growth in the wealth of the average citizen. The result has been a declining birth rate. The result has been trade deficits and budget deficits as far as the eye can see (18 trillion national debt, a similar cumulative trade deficit). The result is growing disparity between the rich and the poor with the development of a police state to enforce those inequalities. The result is foreign ownership of vast amounts of America).

The first and most obvious different approach is to use the prospect of sales in the domestic market as a motivating factor. The main lever that a developed economy has in insuring that investment demand will be located domestically is tariffs on foreign goods. This has several salutary effects.
(1) It causes businesses to invest domestically to meet local demand. This stops the ridiculous situation where the government stimulates the economy to relieve domestic unemployment and the stimulation flows into other lands leaving the market country with debt and ruin and the producing country with the strong economy.
(2) It allows workers wages to rise. If entrepreneurs have to use the local workforce and a boom is created they will bid up salaries.
(3) When the salaries increase, workers will have more money to spend creating more demand. This will allow entrepreneurs to make more money meeting the economic needs of a healthy middle class.

(4) A wealthier society will have stronger environmental protection, better health, and better education.
(5) An emphasis on self sufficiency will lead to greater preparedness in time of war, the ultimate test of civilizations.
(6) It is a source of revenue. This could be used to decrease the payroll and income taxes to increase the competitiveness of the local workers.
(7) It makes the political leaders accountable for the economy. If everything is globalized, the leaders can explain with a straight face that the hard time presently endured by the population is a global phenomena and it has nothing to do with their policies. This excuse will not wash in a national rather than a global economy. (It shouldn't be accepted by the voters even in a free trade economy.)
(8) This makes it more difficult for multinational corporations to hide their profits in low tax jurisdictions.
(9) It makes workplace safety laws easier to enforce.
(10) The decreased volume of foreign trade makes drug smuggling and human trafficking more difficult.

This puts geometry into economic planning. We are using a tariff to construct an economic cell wall / membrane around our country. Like the cells of the body, we will still be affected by what goes on in the other cells / nations of the world but we will be able to no small degree be able to protect our workers from the economic storms that blow around the globe. Lets be clear, our objective is full employment with rising salaries. With a strong enforced border, Keynes equations largely hold. Without a border, trade deficits and immigration make it difficult to raise salaries. In the absence of a strong border, entrepreneurs will attempt with no small degree of success to arbitrage the wage disparity of a wealthy country and a poor country to locate the production in the low wage country and the consumption in the high wage country. They will bring in workers from the low wage country to drive down the wages they have to pay in the wealthy country. This has been seen in a general trend over the last 40 years and is spectacularly illustrated by NAFTA and the trade deficits with China. This is what a reasonable man would predict would happen when opening trade between a poor country and a rich one, and it has been borne out over 40 years of history, 40 years of sustained governmental ineptitude/corruption.

With the use of a tariff, access to the market of a developed country can be limited to businesses within that country and subject to its laws and taxes. Those needs that cannot be met domestically can be met by foreign producers after paying a tariff. This should be high enough to significantly alter business planning -say 40 - 100%. The general drop in international trade will make regulation of trade far easier with much better control of the the border.

To sum, the most powerful tool that a government has in a large developed economy to stimulate domestic investment and a high level of employment is domestic demand. This should be borne in mind at all times. Therefore, access to domestic demand should be regulated to meet the needs of society with a default position of a high tariff.

Footnotes:

1. Taylor Polynomials are named in honor of the English mathematician, Brook Taylor (1685 - 1731).

A function S(t) can be approximated by a power series

$$= S(t_0) + \frac{dS(t_0)}{dt}\frac{(t - t_0)}{1!} + \frac{d^2S(t_0)}{(dt)^2}\frac{(t - t_0)^2}{2!} + \ldots$$

or $s = s_0 + vt + 1/2\ at^2$ to use the familiar high school physics equation. It's interesting that the terms we use for analyzing stocks mathematically fall out of a Taylor polynomial analysis of the money in a company in much the same way that velocity and acceleration fall out of a Taylor polynomial assessment of position .

John Maynard and Lopokova Keynes

Models of Trade Between High and Low Wage Countries

Let's develop a symbolic representation to qualitatively describe the trade between a rich country and a poor country. We will use Keynes basic equation and modify it slightly.
Starting with P = D1 + D2 for supply = demand from worker's wages + from investment demand, let's rename P as prices paid for product (stuff). Then P is a function of stuff (supply) and demand. To emphasize that it is a function, we will relabel P as the function P(s,d). This yields the equation P(s,d) = D1 + D2.

Since our workers are at present spending the vast majority of their salaries, we can substitute (aggregate wages) x (number of workers) for D1. At present we will neglect government revenues/ expenditures to simplify our model.

Let:

P-usa(s,d) = Prices paid for stuff in the rich country.
P-mex(s,d) = Prices paid for stuff in the poor country.
D1usa = Demand from workers' wages in the rich country.
D2usa = Nonwage demand in the rich country.
D1mex = Demand from workers' wages in the poor country.
D2mex = Nonwage demand in the poor country.
Jusa = Jobs in rich country.
Jmex = Jobs in poor country.
Iusa = investment demand (nonwage demand) associated with each job in the rich country.
Imex = investment demand (nonwage demand) associated with each job in the poor country.
Wusa = aggregate wage in rich country.
Wmex = aggregate wage in poor country.

Then our pre NAFTA state can be described as :

P-usa(s,d) = D1usa + D2usa = Wusa x Jusa + Iusa x Jusa .
and
P-mex(s,d) = D1mex + D2mex = Wmex x Jmex +Imex x Jmex.

To treat this as two economies merging into one system we can sum the two equations.

P-usa(s,d) + P-mex(s,d) = Wusa x Jusa + Iusa x Jusa +
Wmex x Jmex + Imex x Jmex.
=D1usa + D2usa + D1mex + D2mex.

Let us further stipulate that for a given level of investment the productivity of the Mexican worker and US worker are roughly comparable (i.e. If you build a high quality US style auto plant the Mexican worker will produce roughly what a US worker would under similar conditions). Let us further stipulate that due to the planned (and historical) destruction of small farmers in Mexico, and the Peso crisis, Mexican wages will not go up with an expansion in the number of Mexican workers. Let us say we then move 700,000 jobs to Mexico.
Let:

P'-usa(s,d) represent our new demand in the US following moving 700,000 jobs to Mexico and

P'-mex(s,d) represent our new demand in Mexico following moving 700,000 jobs to Mexico.

Then we can describe the change as follows:

P'-usa(s,d) = D1usa + D2usa = Wusa x (Jusa-700,000) + Iusa x (Jusa-700,000). and
P'-mex(s,d) = D1mex + D2mex = Wmex x (Jmex + 700,000) +Imex x Jmex + Iusa x 700,000.

with Iusa x 700,000 representing the factories and parts to

moved to Mexico to support the 700000 US jobs that were moved south.

Then our combined equations for the combined economic area are:
P'-usa(s,d) + P'-mex(s,d) = Wusa x (Jusa - 700000) + Iusa x (Jusa -700,000) + Wmex x (Jmex +700,000) + Imex x Jmex. +Iusa x 700,000.
Combining like terms yields
P'-usa(s,d) + P'-mex(s,d) = Wusa x (Jusa - 700000) + Iusa x (Jusa) + Wmex x (Jmex +700,000) + Imex x Jmex.

Then our change in total demand for the NAFTA area is:
(P'-usa(s,d) + P'-mex(s,d))-(Pusa(s,d) +Pmex(s,d) =
=(Wusa x (Jusa - 700000) + Iusa x Jusa) + Wmex x (Jmex +700,000) + Imex x Jmex) -(Wusa x Jusa + Iusa x Jusa + Wmex x Jmex + Imex x Jmex).
= Wusa x (-700,000) + Wmex x (700,000) = - (Wusa -Wmex) x 700,000.

Note:
1. This is an important result. The total demand in the combined area USA + Mexico just dropped by the difference of [(wages paid in USA) - (wages paid in Mexico)] x (number of jobs moved to Mexico).
2. Investment demand is unchanged.
3. Production of "s" stuff is unchanged.

What are the implications of this?

First, it is hugely deflationary. If we take a salary differential of 12.00 / hour in US versus 3.00 per hour in Mexico, 75 % of the demand associated with wages is disappearing. If wage demand is 85 % of the economy, about 66 % of combined wage and investment demand associated with these jobs has disappeared. The drop in demand is concentrated in the US (of course), with 100 % loss in both investment and wage demand. But the Mexican growth in wage demand is a fraction of the US loss (one fourth), so the Mexican total demand grows by 25% consumption demand + 15% investment demand (shifted essentially unchanged from the US) = 40 % of lost US demand. Even if the Mexican workers have a fetish for US products, they simply aren't paid enough to buy them at the previous prices. Note the same amount of stuff is still being produced. There are less dollars chasing the same amount of goods.

Prices then must drop to account for the decreased demand. A drop in prices for businesses with thin margins would be catastrophic, so several things happen. First, in response to the market signal of decreased prices, production will be curtailed, primarily involving layoffs in the more well paid workers in the developed country. Second, the government will respond to the deflationary pressure with a monetary expansion to save the jobs of the workers to the extent possible, to increase price stability, and to keep the banking system solvent. This also benefits those close to government by allowing the government to print money without a massive inflation or hyperinflation. This is a huge allocation of power to the government and the financial centers. The illusion is created that the government is staving off disaster by intervening, when in fact the open economy policies they are pursuing are running the country into the ground.

Second, in the short run it offers large profits to entrepreneurs who can use the demand in the rich country and source in the poor country. These profits will decrease due to competition and price collapse due to decreasing demand, but initially fortunes will be made for a few.

Third, as production is curtailed in the rich country to bring production in line with demand, additional workers will be laid off in the rich country. Combined investment demand for the two countries will be dramatically impacted to the downside as the money to buy stuff disappears. This will lead to a further drop in demand continuing a downward cascade. Taken to a theoretical conclusion, all the jobs in the rich country could be moved to the poor country. As above, this would lead to a 60% drop in initial demand related to these jobs for the combined NAFTA area. However and worse, this drop in demand will lead rapidly to a drop in investment demand, since the market to sell into has disappeared.

If, initially the rich country's demand accounted for 3/4 of total demand in the NAFTA region, moving the jobs to the poor country would initially cause a drop in total demand of 60% x .75 = 45 %. A commensurate drop in investment demand would then lay off almost half of the remaining workers (now located in the poor country). (Since we only need to produce 55% of what we previously needed to produce, we can close almost half the redundant factories). This would of course cut demand almost in half again. And so on. Other factors such a massive budget deficit supervene to damp this slide off a cliff but the downward pressure of deflationary collapse is there.

Let's define:

1) Primary loss of jobs - direct loss of jobs due to the job being moved to the poor country.
2) Secondary loss of jobs - loss of jobs due to the reduction in wage demand caused by moving the job from the rich country to the poor country.
3) Tertiary loss of jobs- loss of jobs due reduction in demand caused by the secondary loss of jobs.

Fourth, our arguments have so far held wages constant in the poor country and rich country. This is emphatically not what will be going on in the real world. As additional workers are laid off, forced to take salary cuts, cuts in vacation, and cuts in benefits, demand falls further. The ongoing pressure shifts the wage discussion from "What kind of a raise can you give me?" to "Can I please keep my job? As workers are less valued, communication between workers and management will suffer leading to worse and more dangerous working conditions. Less attention will be paid to increasing productivity and quality and more on keeping costs in line by moving jobs to a cheaper location.

The math for the workers taking a 50% wage cut in the rich country is almost the same as moving the jobs to a country with a salary scale one half of the rich country. The main difference is the investment demand in the 50% wage cut is domestic and the investment demand in the jobs outsourced to China is in China. Otherwise, the decrease in demand is mathematically similar.

Lets see what happens if our industrialist doesn't want to move to Mexico or fly to Vietnam to supervise his factory. He can use immigration to reduce wages here at home. (Live in Beverley Hills, run a sweatshop in LA). In 1984 meatpacking workers in Austin, Minnesota were making what had been an industry standard of 10.69 / hour which adjusted for inflation would be 24.30. Since that time immigration has led to a decrease in these wages so that meat processing jobs now pay 12 - 15 dollars per hour, a 30 - 50 % wage cut. To simplify our calculation, lets say immigration drops salary in meatpacking from 24.30 to 13.50 which is a good ballpark estimate. This is a 45% wage cut.

Then if D1 (wage demand) initially is 85 % of P(s,d) and D2 is 15% of P(s,d), what happens when a 100,000 meatpackers take a 45% wage cut?

Then our initial condition is : P(s,d) = D1+ D2
and our final condition is:
P'(s,d)
= D1- 100,000 x (24.30 - 13.50) x 2000 hours/year + D2
= D1- 100,000 x 10.8 x 2000 + D2 = D1- 100,000 x 21,600 + D2
Subtracting: Change in demand P(s,d) - P'(s,d) = -100,000 workers each taking a 21,600 wage cut/year per worker = 2.16 billion.

If our entrepreneurs have imported 10 million workers to hold down wages and they have a similar chilling effect on incomes elsewhere, this could result in a reduction in demand across the United States of 216 billion. In a 17 trillion dollar economy this would represent about a 1.3 % contraction in demand directly. This is obviously a rough estimate. The loss of demand would result in the loss of 1.52 million jobs; when these people can't shop, demand would fall further leading to another 330,000 people losing their jobs. When these people can't shop we lose another 7000 jobs. Net result - 10 million jobs are reduced significantly in salary and 1.9 million people are unemployed.

To continue our story problems, if there is a 340 billion trade deficit with China, the factory wage in China is 2.20 per hour, the trade deficit causes the direct loss of 2.39 million jobs, what is the secondary loss in demand? The loss in domestic US demand directly calculated is the loss of wages + loss of investment associated with investment. If wage demand would be 85% of the costs associated with those jobs, then we can multiply wages by 1.18 to compensate for this.
So 2.39 million jobs x 2000 hours x 1.18 x 13.50/hour = 76,145 million = 76.1 billion. (The loss of demand in the combined area of China and US would be 2.39 million jobs x

2000 hours/job x (13.50 - 2.20)/hour = 54.0 billion. - a slight additional boost for China, a significant loss for the US). This loss of 76.1 billion corresponds to a loss of an additional loss of 535,000 jobs.

535,000 x 2000 hours x 1.18 x 13.50 = 17.0 billion loss in demand caused by loss of respending by the secondary job loss. This would lead to the loss of another 119,000 jobs. The reduction in demand associated with this job loss would lead to an additional loss of 27,000 jobs. The loss in respending associated with these jobs would cause an additional 6,000 job loss. These estimates of respending job losses is conservative. Adding up these losses 535,000 + 119,000 + 27,000 + 6,000 = 687,000 additional jobs lost. So our trade deficit with China costs at least 3.1 million jobs, not 2.39 million (which is still way too many).

Lamprey Capitalism

How China gets it done.

China has had phenomenal growth since the year 2000. Let us build a mathematical model which describes this. Then we can study their successes and our failures more thoroughly.

China has directed the trade between the US and her so that there has been a positive balance of trade for China. There have been a variety of tools at the Dragon's disposal (and China has used them), but the main tool has been a severe under valuation of her currency. To really model what is going on we will need expanded equations that allow us to follow the money.

Initially we have two countries with relatively separate economies, the US and China.

Borrowing from our previous work, let:

Photo above from Great Lakes Fishery Commission shows parasitic sea lamprey feeding on American lake trout.

P-usa(s,d) = Prices paid for stuff in US.
P-chi(s,d) = Prices paid for stuff in China.
D1usa = Demand from workers wages in US.
D2usa = Private demand not directly related to workers wages in US.
DGusa = Demand from government spending in the US - net. (i.e. deficit government spending).
D1chi = Demand from workers wages in China.
D2chi = Private demand not directly related to workers wages in China.
DGchi = Demand from net government spending in China (i.e. deficit chinese government spending).
g).
Jusa = Jobs in US.
Jchi = Jobs in China.
Iusa = Private investment demand (nonwage demand associated with each job US).
Ichi = Private investment demand (nonwage demand associated with each job in China).
Wusa = Aggregate wage in US.
Wchi = Aggregate wage in China.

C = Costs.
S = Sales.
Jent = Jobs moved by entrepreneur.
Pent = Profits made by entrepreneur.

During the cold war with two separate economies the economies can be described as:

P-usa(s,d) = D1usa + D2usa + DGusa= Wusa x Jusa + Iusa x Jusa + DGusa and
P-chi(s,d) = D1chi + D2chi + DGchi = Wchi x Jchi + Ichi x Jchi + DGchi

Two separate systems.

Now the Chinese government decides to enter the world trading system. They undervalue their currency by a factor of 6. This allows them to have a positive balance of trade. So our capitalist entrepreneur decides to make money sourcing product using cheap wages in China and selling in the US (Plantation Capitalism plan). His costs "C" for a given amount of product that he sells in US can be estimated at:

C = Salary costs + non salary costs = 1/6 Wusa x J(entrepreneur) + Iusa x Jentrepreneur.

Now if the salary is 85% of the cost of the US product, cutting this by a factor of 6 makes the wage cost of the product .167 of its original cost and the total cost adding back in the 15% not due to wages would give a price of .167 + .15 = ~ 32%. Thus our entrepreneur can initially cut his costs by 2/3 and most of this drops directly to the bottom line. Even better for him, this is offshore and he can hide much of his profit from the taxman. Initially, this does not destroy the demand schedule, so the price he sells the product for does not plummet immediately. Soon, however, competition begins to erode his profit margin and demand also begins to drop because the now unemployed American workers are buying less. Note that initially up to 2/3 of the sale of Chinese products doesn't actually go to China but ends up as profit for the multinational business. Where does this money go? Who knows? When the profits of Apple from selling stuff made in China end up in Ireland it points to the extreme flexibility companies have in hiding this money from the tax man. Is only 5.00 of Wal-Mart's 150 dollar sales per share profit? Let's leave our plantation capitalist behind for now although the shadow world of offshore banking needs to be explored more thoroughly. (Actually in this environment, our capitalist has to move production to where it is cheap or by and large he will be out of business - that's how the rules have been set up.)

China has to maintain this artificially low currency. How do they do that? They print their currency, the Yuan. This of course drives down the price of the Yuan. They can do this and spend the printed currency ("quantitative easing") on infrastructure or other government priorities, some better conceived than others. Most of the money they print they use to mop up the foreign currency (dollars) that accumulate from trade flows. This drives the dollar up and the Yuan down to the desired level. With the dollars they buy assets. They have bought US treasuries, gold and other precious metals, companies, farmland, influence throughout Africa and South America. Their purchase of treasuries sets up a sick cycle where we purchase goods from China at an artificially low price and they loan us our money back again so we can do it again. This contributed to the rapid expansion of debt in the Bush Presidency. Conversely, this plan is associated with a rapid expansion of the Yuan which has been enormously stimulative to the Chinese economy, making China the current economic wonder of the world.

If 1,000,000 jobs are moved to China, and 85% of the costs related to those jobs in the US is salary, and the 15% of nonwage costs related to those jobs is also sourced in China after the move (in real life this number would be more flexible), the equations after this perturbation would look something like this:

P-usa(s,d) = D1usa + D2usa + DGusa= Wusa x (Jusa -1,000,000) + Iusa x (Jusa - 1,000,000) + DGusa and

P-chi(s,d) = D1chi + D2chi + DGchi = Wchi x (Jchi +1,000,000) + Ichi x Jchi + 1,000,000 x Iusa) +DGchi

Now our entrepreneur has moved his product to the US, so the same amount of goods is present, but the salary demand in the US is decreased. As shown elsewhere, much of this deficit has been funded by government borrowing or money printing, but there is some downward pressure on prices.

The Chinese mop up the dollars by printing money roughly equal to the entrepreneurs' spending in China, 1,000,000 workers x the Chinese wage + nonwage expenses associated with production or 1,000,000 x (Wchi + Iusa). They then buy the dollars and spend them on a mix of US treasury bonds (more of these several years ago, less now), gold, silver, farmland, resource stocks, etc.

The additional hiring stimulates the Chinese economy causing additional growth by respending. (The 1,000,000 US jobs initially moved to China will cause additional jobs to be created to serve the needs of these workers).

The US must borrow to maintain spending. US demand is decreased by [1,000,000 x (Wusa + Iusa)]. If the entrepreneur lives in the US, he may have considerable profit which he can put back into demand if he lives like an oligarch; in the above example this could be 5/6 of what would be the American wages of his workers if he still had US workers. Or he could live in Bangkok and send nothing to the US beyond manufactured products from China. Most likely he lives in the US and puts his money in an offshore business entity. For many years the Chinese bought a lot of treasury bonds which would boost demand. As foreign demand for treasuries has diminished, the US government has turned to quantitative easing to stave off deflationary collapse of the US economy.

If the Chinese spent their entire trade surplus on US treasuries, this could be represented by the following equation:
P-usa(s,d) = D1usa + D2usa + DGusa
= Wusa x (Jusa -1,000,000) + Iusa x (Jusa - 1,000,000) + DGusa (Of which 1,000,000 x (Wchi + Iusa) is a loan from China to suppress the Chinese wage scale/currency) and

P-chi(s,d) = D1chi + D2chi + DGchi = Wchi x (Jchi +1,000,000) + Ichi x Jchi + 1,000,000 x Iusa) +DGchi
= Wchi x Jchi + Ichi x Jchi + 1,000,000 x (Wchi + Iusa) +DGchi

Note again that the Chinese trade surplus is 1,000,000 x (Wchi +Iusa) and the US trade deficit is larger at 1,000,000 x (Wusa + Iusa)
or if the Chinese wage is 1/6 the US wage the difference between the Chinese trade surplus and the US trade deficit is 1,000,000 x 5/6 Wusa, or the equivalent of 5/6 of the wages of the workers who were laid off. This is available (if demand is artificially maintained by government spending) for profit for our entrepreneur. Mega profits. Huge win for Plantation Capitalists. The entrepreneurs/Plantation Capitalists are making truly massive profits. (To paraphrase Mel Brooks in Spaceballs, they are not doing it for the money, they're doing it for a s--tload of money!)

Note again ......if the Chinese wage is 1/6 the US wage, the difference between the Chinese trade surplus and the US trade deficit is ..... the equivalent of 5/6 of the wages of the workers who were laid off. This is available (if demand is

artificially maintained by government spending) for profit for our entrepreneur. Mega profits.
Huge win for plantation capitalists.

Our trade deficit can be larger than the Chinese trade surplus with the difference available for our Plantation Capitalist entrepreneur as an offshore (largely untaxed) profit!

Note in the graph below that the Chinese figures are indeed lower than the US figures by about 100 billion. This is going to Plantation Capitalist Profit offshore. It's one third of our deficit with China (and that is just numbers we have access to). It is untaxed profit on an epic scale.

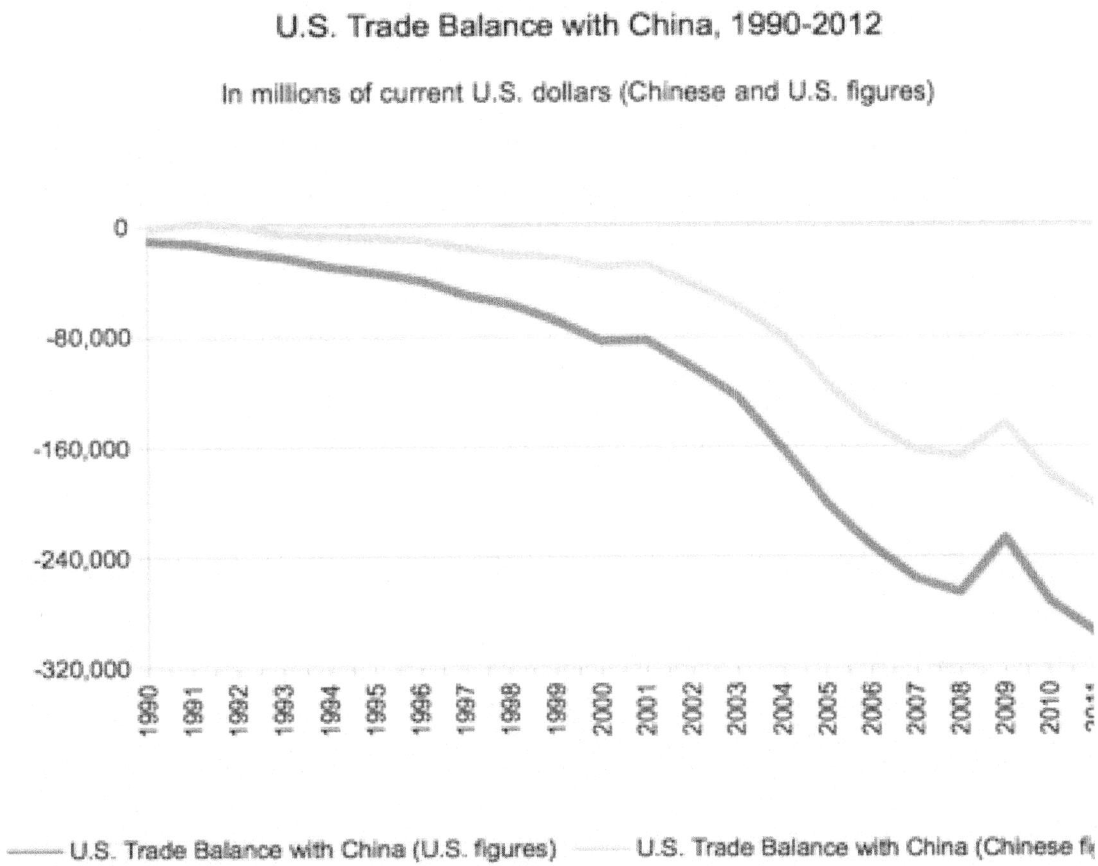

Further note that initially (the left hand side of the curve)

the trade deficit of the US was a multiple of the Chinese surplus. A verification of our theory.

This is obviously painful for the American worker whose salary is diminished and whose government is bankrupt.

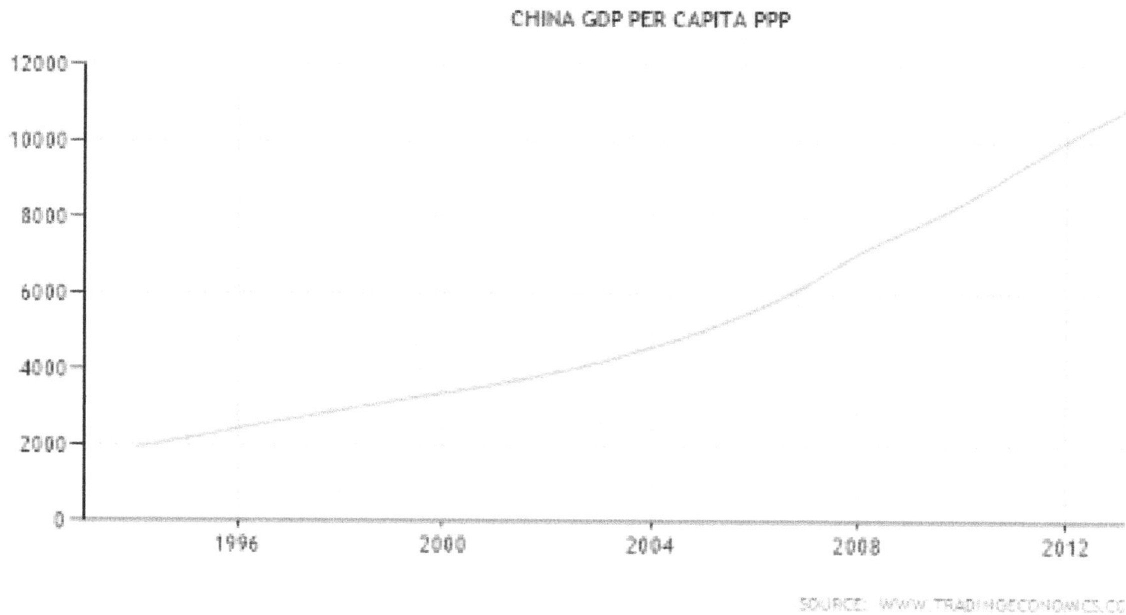

The Chinese GDP per capita has grown by a factor of 6 (600%) since 1993- a growth rate of just over 9% per year. This is a successful mercantilist plan well executed for over 20 years by China's leaders.

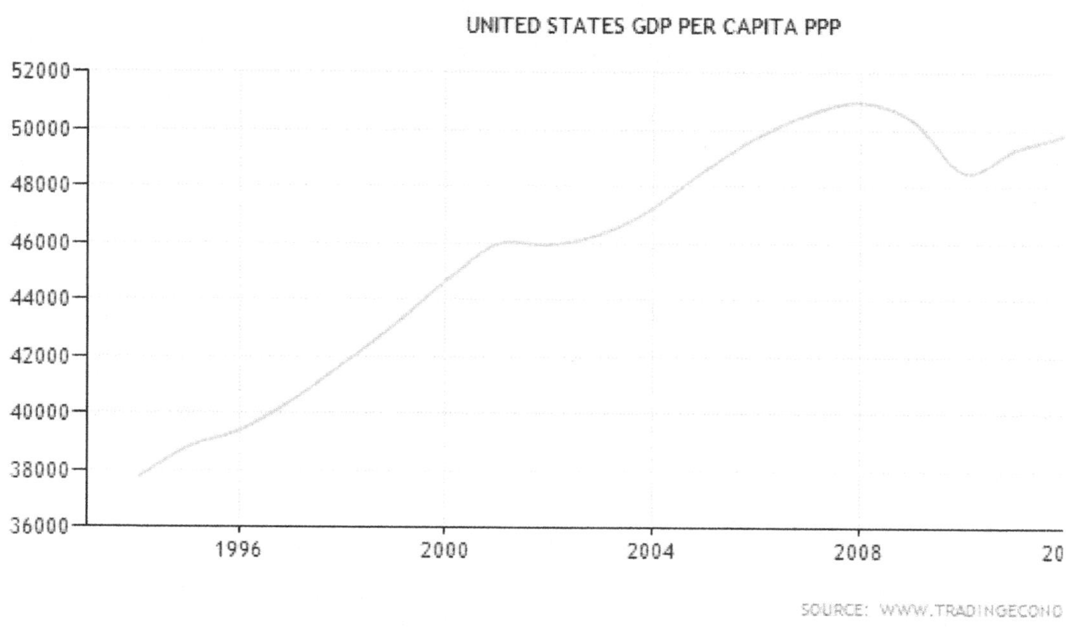

The US GDP per capita has increased by .34 (34%) over 20 years, 1.47% a year. The work of real men of genius educated by the best educational system in the world. While it is true that over the twenty year period the gentlemen from China beat them by a factor of 6/.34 = 17.6, and the Chinese treasury is full and ours is at negative 18.2 trillion, our Harvard and Yale educated elites did it the "right" way, for which we say, "Bravo!"

The Mexican GDP per capita increased by .23 (23%) over 20 years. 1.1% a year. Poor Mexico. So far from God, so near the US. They (and we) deserve better. With different management their results should have paralleled the Chinese. This is a control graph. A Free Trade advocate will say that the Chinese growth is due to starting from a low base. However, this curve shows that Mexico, with a hardworking low wage young workforce achieved results that can best be described as mediocre and actually worse than the US under a regime of Free Trade.

Actually, the question really isn't how does China get it done. Their game plan is simple and so far punishingly effective. The real question why do we let them do it to us. The answer probably lies with game theory. The rewards of this system (in the US) are very concentrated and huge (the Plantation Capitalists do very well sourcing product in China and selling in the US market) and the losses tend to be diffuse (although if you lose your job it may be catastrophic). This allows the Plantation Capitalists resources to lobby/corrupt the government to not defend the economy. The individual worker tightening his belt doesn't have the resources to bribe politicians to see it his way.

One's initial thought is the Chinese are the lamprey, sucking the vitality out of the American lake trout; but deeper thinking on the subject suggests that the true lampreys in this situation are the Plantation Capitalists/ multinational corporations selfishly causing pain and misery as they feed on their hosts, the American people.

NAFTA

MEXICO

"So far from God, so near the United States."
- Porfirio Diaz

Hernando Cortez conquered Mexico in 1519. Mexico was ruled as a Spanish colony until the 19th century. During the Napoleonic wars, Mexico began a struggle for independence 1810-1821. The Treaty of Cordoba (1821) established Mexico as a sovereign state. There was a short period of monarchy from 1821-1823. The Republic of Mexico was established with a federal constitution in 1824.

The political history of Mexico continued to be turbulent in the first half of the 19th century and was dominated by Antonio Lopez de Santa Anna. Mexico lost over half its territory to the United States in the Texas Revolution of 1836 and the US provoked Mexican American war of 1848. Santa Anna was ousted by Mexican liberals. They wrote the Constitution of 1857 which established the principles of equality before the law, separation of church and state, and removed special privileges for the Catholic Church and various indigenous communities. This caused a war between the liberals and the conservatives. The liberals won the war, but they went into foreign debt to do so.

On 7/17/1861 Benito Juarez, President of Mexico, suspended payments on debts accumulated in the reform war. This angered France, Britain, and Spain which were major creditors. Napoleon III made the case to go to war on free trade principles. (Foolish ideas multiplied like rabbits in the mind of Napoleon III. He was also apprehensive about the growth of US power, which while a theoretical concern for France was not really as immediate a problem as Bismarck right next door.) He wanted access to the Mexican market for French goods, and he wanted access to Mexican sliver.

The United States was wracked by the Civil War, so France, England, and Spain invaded Mexico. When the British and Spanish realized France wanted all of Mexico, they wisely left. The French installed Maximilian I as Emperor. This continued until the end of the American Civil War at which point the US was free to enforce the Monroe Doctrine, and the French left. In 1867 Republican leadership under Benito Juarez was reestablished in Mexico City, and Maximilian was executed.

Benito Juarez controversially used presidential power to assure reelection in 1867 and 1872. He died in office in 1872 of a heart attack. Juarez was succeeded by Sebastian Lerdo de Tejeda. In 1876 when Lerdo attempted reelection, Porfirio Diaz revolted and took power which he held until 1911. Initially he was a liberal, but the need for power led him to become a dictator. (He had actually been mentored in law school by Benito Juarez and he was a hero of the war against the French.) He had an armed police force under his control, the *Rurales* (paramilitary force in the hinterland), and other forces of state coercion. These he used to intimidate voters and win elections (or fraudulently steal elections). Freedom of the Press was also dispensed with.

Mexico industrialized rapidly under his rule (the Porfiriato) which guaranteed property rights to foreign investors with a great increase in infrastructure. The capitalism concentrated wealth and power in a few families. Large foreign companies from the US, UK, and France had great power while majority of people worked as serfs on great estates or poorly paid workers. Land reform begun under previous leaders such as Juarez was undone reducing the small farmers. No peasant or farmer could claim the land they worked without formal legal title. 95% of the land was owned by less than 5% of the population. Workers on the large plantations were often beaten for minor offenses. Murders of workers by their masters was common. Debts were passed down from generation to generation. (Plantation Capitalism)

This explosive mix contributed to the Mexican Revolution. This was a 10 year struggle (1910-1920). One tenth of the population died (worse than the American Civil War). The Revolution ended the system of large landed estates (haciendas) that dated back to the Spanish Conquest. The Constitution of 1917 decreased individual property rights and empowered the State to expropriate owners. It also gave the mineral rights to the State which laid the groundwork for the formation of Pemex, the state oil company. Organized labor was recognized in Article 123, guaranteeing labor union rights.

In 1929 the organization that soon became the PRI (Partido Revolucionario Instiutional) was formed. This party ran Mexico until the election of Vincinte Fox in 2000. It's running Mexico now.

President Lazaro Cardenas passed the 1934 Agrarian Code. He redistributed 45,000,0000 acres including 4,000,000acres of American owned land. Cardenas distributed more land than all previous land reform put together. Production increased as large estates were reduced. According to these reforms, an *ejido* would be established if the government saw fit which would give landless farmers the right to work a small tract of land (ejido) - essentially use rights provided they did not fail to use the land for more than two years. They could pass the rights on to their children. However, they did not actually own the land. Cardenas nationalized the oil industry in 1938.

In 1970 President Luis Echeverria initially tried to stop land reform, but outcry from the peasants forced him to change course. He then expropriated foreign owned farms which were converted into communal ejidos.

President Miguel de la Madrid succeeded president Lopez Portillo in December 1982. He had been Lopez Portillo's planning minister from 1976 to 1982 and had watched the debt quadruple during that period. It was now 85 billion dollars and he and his planning minister, Carlos Salinas, began emphasizing the need for austerity/ belt tightening. He also tried to attack corruption. Unfortunately, he had difficulty walking the walk. There is a tradition in PRI politics (the above mentioned Cardenas is an exception) that the President leaves office rich. Lopez Portillo was granted immunity and left office with a fortune estimated at 1 billion dollars. In May 1984 Jack Anderson leaked a CIA report that De la Madrid had already stashed 162 million dollars in the Cayman Islands. (Not bad work if you can get it- 162 million / 18 months on the job = 9 million of corrupt looting per month!) The US State Department simply commented,"US Government applauds President de la Madrid's commitment to address the issue of honesty in government."[1]

He did prosecute Arturo Durazo Moreno, a childhood friend of Lopez Portillo. Durazo became Portillo's personal security chief and became head of the Mexico City Police when Portillo became president in spite of the fact he had been indicted by a US grand jury on narcotics 11 months earlier. He converted the Mexico City police into a criminal/ drug empire. His house in Mexico City is now a corruption museum; his house in Zihuatanejo was a full scale replica of the Parthenon with 500 marble statues. He served 6 years of a 16 year sentence.

The 1988 Mexican presidential election pitted Carlos Salinas de Gortari, the hand picked successor of Miguel de la Madrid and the PRI, against Cuauhtemoc Cardenas, the PRI's governor Michoacan State and son of Lazlo Cardenas (who nationalized the oil industry in the 1930's and passed the 1934 Agrarian Code redistributing land to the peasants). Cardenas was representing the National Democratic Front, which had a job creation program which it wanted to pay for with a repudiation of the Mexican debt. Salinas, a Harvard trained free marketeer, ran on free trade, honoring the debt, and other neoliberal policies.

On July 6 after the polls closed the Mexican people waited for the election return. Manual Bartlett, the man overseeing the vote, announced that the Federal Election Commission's computer system had crashed which would delay the result. A week later, they declared Salinas the winner. Of course, the computer system hadn't crashed. The PRI had simply stolen the election.

This was confirmed in Miguel de la Madrid's autobiography published in 2004. *Computing,* a UK technology magazine, interviewed data entry operators who were working the election. Here is what Adolfo Onofre, one the workers who was there related about what actually happened:

> "We arrived at work on the morning of July 6, election day, at the central computer and statistic official. When we got there we discovered that the rooms were empty and our computers weren't there. We were ordered into a minibus and taken to the Government House (in Mexico City), to a room with blacked out windows. Our computers had been set up there, complete with the voter database. We started to enter the data. As the supervisors saw that Salinas was losing, they ordered us to leave aside votes for the PRI and only enter the opposition votes. Then, at about 3 A.M. on July 7, the supervisor called a halt, and with tears in his eyes, he told us: If you care for your families, your jobs, and your lives, enter all votes from now on in favor of the PRI. I went back to work and did as I was told. I wanted to cry but I had to do it.
>
> They kept us there until five or six in the evening the following day. When I'd finished my work, I called up the voting record for my uncle, and to my astonishment the computer record showed that he, an opposition supporter, had voted for Salinas. That was when I realized why we had been told only to enter opposition votes in the beginning. While we were away from the

computers, they had reversed all the data from the first session of data capture so all those votes showed up as Salinas votes."[2]

There are additional sources pointing to a fraudulent election (although if the ex President of Mexico states the PRI fixed the election, you don't need a whole lot more evidence). Jose Berberan et al, Radiografia del Fraude: Analisis de los dates oficiales del 6 de julio (Mexico City: Editorial Nuestro Tiempo, 1988), 153pp ("X-Ray of Fraud: Analysis of official data about July 6")

"The statisticians found two telltale signs of massive tampering. In place of the bell shaped curve that would be expected to describe the distribution of votes obtained by each party, the PRI was found to have two such curves: one centered around a mean of 36% (its true national average), and the other peaking around an implausible 100 %."

"A second diagnostic test revealed the provenance of these 'unanimous' results. Whereas totals for each of the opposition parties had last digits that occurred with roughly equal frequency, the last digit of PRI totals was 60% more likely to be a zero, indicating that the PRI had inflated its totals by simply adding zeros to its actual vote count."

"In Guerrero, the opposition tabulated 80.5% of the votes on the basis of copies of official tally sheets. It counted 359,369 votes for Cardenas and 90,796 for Salinas. When the official vote count was released, Salinas wound up with 309,202 and Cardenas with 182,872."

This last fits with the computer operators report that the votes had been switched.

The international business community (bankers who were none to keen on a debt default) and the Reagan administration recognized the election immediately. Hernandez Galicia, the head of the oil workers union did not. For forty years these had been the best paid workers in Mexico. It was a deeply corrupt union in a deeply corrupt state; the output per worker was only 1/3 of the output per worker in Venezuela. Galicia charged that de La Madrid's director of Pemex, Mario Ramon Beteta, had stolen money from a tanker deal much like his predecessor, Jorge Diaz Serrano. (Serrano was George H. W. Bush former business partner at Zapata Oil and the former head of Pemex under President Lopez Portillo. He owned a mansion on the golf course in Vail, Colorado. Serrano was convicted of stealing a 34 million commission on two oil tankers and served 5 years. 300 million barrels went missing during Serrano's tenure so the level of crime was far higher (30 dollars / barrel x 300 million barrels~ roughly 9 billion dollars.) The union began to buy automatic weapons. This was a threat to the integrity of Mexico since the union outnumbered the Mexican Army.

Salinas responded. In January 1989, a bazooka blew down Galicia's front door and he was taken to jail in his underwear. 43 other oil workers union officials were charged with crimes that included murder, arms trafficking, and gangsterism. Several hundred Uzi machine guns were confiscated. When the accounts of these men were examined, they had 3.2 billion dollars deposited in Citibank, Chase, MHT, and Bank of America. Salinas continued to crush dissent jailing the head of Aeromexico's union, the head of the social security system's union,and the heads of a Mexico City bus lines union. All of these businesses were privatized.[3] The stolen election was justified by force, not righteousness.

Salinas tried to restructure the Mexican debt, but this

produced only minor benefits (7 billion dollar reduction). He then tried full implementation of a neoliberal agenda. He sold off public assets in telecommunications,steel, airlines, and banking and used the 24 billion dollar proceeds from the fire sale to service Mexico's debt. He opened the economy up to foreigners. He helped put an end to the constitutional right to *ejidos* (communally held land), undermining the agrarian reform of Lazaro Cardenas. And he negotiated the NAFTA treaty with George H W Bush in 1992. The treaty pushed through the US Congress by President Bill Clinton in 1993.

Trade liberalization unleashed increased drug trafficking. Mexico's role in drug exports had been growing since the mid 1980's when Columbia's traditional routes through Florida came under increasing interdiction. Raul Salinas, Jr (Carlos Salinas' older brother, i.e. the Presidents older brother) had bank accounts in Citibank, Rothschild, Julius Baer, Banque Genevoise de Gestion, Bank Cremi, the Cayman Islands, London, New York, Germany, and Luxembourg. On November 15, 1998 Raul's wife, Paulina Castanon, was halted when she tried to withdraw 84 million from Bank Pictet in Geneva. A Swiss prosecutor concluded at least 70 million of this had come from drug deals. In January 1999, Raul Salinas was sentenced to fifty years in prison(reduced to 27 years) for his role in the 1994 murder of his brother in law, Jose Francisco Ruiz Massieu. [4] (This was later overturned).

The wholesale Mexican drug trade is estimated to be between 13.6 - 49.4 billion dollars per year. By the end of Felipe Calderon's administration (President of Mexico 2006-2012), the official death toll in the Mexican Drug War was at least 60,000. Estimates set the death toll above 120,000, not including 27,000 missing! Drug cartels in Mexico control 70% of foreign narcotics entering the US.

In March 1994 Luis Donoldo Colosio, the PRI candidate for president, was assassinated. Salinas then chose Ernesto Zedillo to be his successor. During this time Mexico was having a temporary economic boom based on borrowing and government spending. A devaluation of the peso was delayed until after the election. Mexico took on a huge amount of debt. The debt of Mexico's private banks rose from 8 to 15.5 billion from 1991 to 1994 denominated in dollars. Many of these bankers were political insiders who didn't know much about banking and the loans were of poor quality. 28 billion of Mexico's 100 billion debt was in high yield short term Mexican dollar bonds, Tesobonos. All this short term debt allowed the Mexican economy to briefly look good right before the 1994 election and Zedillo won in August 1994.

Then the wheels came off the wagon in the "Tequila Crisis". In December 1994, the Peso was devalued. Unfortunately, once it started dropping, it just kept plummeting. Capital outflows had started after Colosio was assasinated, but once confidence was lost in December, it became a torrent. Interest rates were raised to 30% to try to keep capital in the country. The 33 billion dollar reserve that had been built up over the Salinas Presidency vaporized. Unemployment rose to 28% and real wages fell 25 %. 40% of Mexico's 86,000 small businesses went bankrupt. Several hundred thousand individuals went bankrupt. [5] Agriculture in Mexico also changed during this period with the number of Mexicans employed in rural agriculture declining from 8.1 million to 6.8 million- an internal displacement of 1.3 million workers. This rural urban migration would put downward pressure on urban salaries (this agricultural disruption also fueled emigration to the US). Small farmers (peasants) on farms 12 acres or less had the hardest time competing with subsidized mechanized large US farms. <u>In 2000 more than half the population was surviving on less than four dollars per day, and the middle class had been destroyed.</u>

Unsurprisingly, 1995 - 2003 were record years for illegal immigration. Mexico today has huge problems with over borrowing, capital flight, corruption, money laundering, and narcotics, and violence. The regular jobs still pay terribly as the multinational corporations practice Plantation Capitalism.

NAFTA
US PERSPECTIVE

Prior to the implementation of NAFTA, Al Gore, Vice President of the United States had a debate with Ross Perot on national TV about the merits of the agreement. Al Gore predicted NAFTA would lead to greater prosperity and blamed the Smoot Hawley Act for the Great Depresssion, implying that tariffs or protectionism was boneheaded. This has been the established neoliberal academic position. Ross Perot, a businessman and a billionaire, predicted that NAFTA would cause a giant sucking sound of American jobs being moved to Mexico. Mr. Perot lost the debate rhetorically that night, but the experiment has now been run and the results were analyzed by Robert E. Scott in his paper, Heading South, U.S.-Mexico trade and job displacement after NAFTA(2011). Here are his main findings:

• The United States had a small ($1.6 billion) trade surplus with Mexico (supporting 29,400 jobs) in 1993, the year before NAFTA took effect.
• U.S. trade deficits with Mexico as of 2010 displaced production that could have supported 682,900 U.S. jobs; given the pre-NAFTA trade surplus, all of those jobs have been lost or displaced since NAFTA. This estimate of 682,900 net jobs displaced takes into account the additional jobs created by exports to Mexico.
• Rapidly growing trade deficits and job displacement happened as a

surge of foreign direct investment (FDI) poured into Mexico from private investors (NAFTA made it attractive to companies all over the world to invest in Mexico to gain duty free access to the U.S. market). FDI tripled as a share of Mexico's gross domestic product in the post-NAFTA period and fueled the outsourcing of jobs and production to Mexico.

• Most of the jobs displaced by trade with Mexico as of 2010 were in manufacturing industries (415,000 jobs; 60.8% of the total jobs displaced).

• Computer and electronic parts (150,300 jobs, 22% of the 682,900 displaced jobs) and motor vehicles and parts (108,000 jobs; 15.8% of the total) were the manufacturing industries hardest hit by growing bilateral trade deficits.

• More jobs were created in Mexico (30,400) by the growth of net exports of autos and auto parts to the United States in 2010 than were created in the entire U.S. auto industry in the same period, which added only 25,700 jobs between December 2009 and December 2010. The 30,400 jobs displaced in autos and parts in 2010 explains more than one-quarter of all jobs displaced by the growth of trade deficits with Mexico between 2007 and 2010 (116,400 jobs).

• The 682,900 jobs displaced as of 2010 were distributed across all 50 states, the District of Columbia, and Puerto Rico. The 10 hardest-hit states (i.e., jobs displaced as a share of total state employment) were Michigan (43,600 jobs lost, 1.0%), Indiana (24,400, 0.8%), Kentucky (12,100, 0.6%), Ohio (34,900, 0.6%), Tennessee (16,400, 0.6%), New Hampshire (4,000, 0.6%), Illinois (34,700, 0.6%), Alabama (11,100, 0.6%), Massachusetts (17,100, 0.5%), and Texas (55,600, 0.5%).

• The states with the most jobs displaced were California (86,500 jobs), Texas (55,600), Michigan (43,600), Ohio (34,900), Illinois (34,700), New York (34,300), Florida (28,800), Pennsylvania (26,300), Indiana (24,400), and North Carolina (18,900).

• The hardest-hit congressional districts, as a share of total

employment, had large numbers of workers displaced by manufacturing trade, especially in autos, auto bodies, and parts, and in computer and electronic parts production.
Half of the top 20 hardest-hit districts were in Michigan, followed by four in California, three in Indiana, two in Ohio, and one in Texas.

The balance of trade with Mexico went from being a slight surplus in 1993 to being a trade deficit of -16.6 billion in 1997, a trade deficit of -34.3 billion in 2000, a trade deficit of -90.8 billion in 2007, and a trade deficit of - 97.2 billion in 2010 (note all of these estimates leave out the 13.6- 49.4 billion dollar drug trade). Not only were 682, 900 jobs lost, but the remaining workers were subjected to the threat of their job being moved leading to a loss of bargaining power for workers contributing to a loss of wages.

This is an underestimate of the damage. 845,000 US manufacturing workers have applied for Trade Adjustment Assistance (TAA) because they lost their jobs due to imports from Canada or Mexico or the relocation of their factories to those countries. The TAA program is narrow and this is therefore an undercount. US workers without a college degree have lost 12.2% of their wages since NAFTA was passed. Real wages in Mexico have fallen significantly below pre NAFTA levels since price increases have exceeded wage increases. A minimum wage earner in Mexico has sustained a 38% wage decrease since NAFTA in real terms.

NAFTA made Mexico a safer place to invest and lowered the costs of doing business in Mexico. It gave Mexican investment access to the U.S. market, access to cheap Mexican labor, improved intellectual property rights, more lax enforcement of labor and environmental laws. Foreign direct investment nearly tripled from 1.0% GDP prior to NAFTA to 2.9% after NAFTA.

NAFTA did more. It required Mexico to dismantle much of the social safety net. Prior to running the experiment, proponents of NAFTA predicted this would lead to a prosperous Mexican middle class. This did not materialize. Partly this was due to the Peso crisis of 1994. The Peso was depreciated through the end of the 1990's .This led to greater exports and helped Mexican export industries. The depreciation led to a 15.5% decline in real income for the Mexican worker by 1996 with modest improvement since that time. Mexican development has been very uneven with northern states of Mexico with a higher level of skills and infrastructure benefiting more from NAFTA than poorer regions of Mexico.

Agriculture in Mexico also changed during this period with the number of Mexicans employed in rural agriculture declining from 8.1 million to 6.8 million- an internal displacement of 1.3 million workers which is greater than the number of American jobs lost. This rural urban migration put downward pressure on urban salaries and fueled emigration to the US). Small farmers (peasants) on farms 12 acres or less had the hardest time competing with subsidized mechanized large US farms. Before NAFTA, Mexico spent 1.8 billion on food imports. Now it spends 24 billion. Up to one fifth of Mexican children do not have proper nutrition.

The North American Free Trade Agreement has negatively impacted American workers in a number of ways.

Jeff Faux wrote on 12/9/2013:

> "North American Free Trade Agreement (NATFA) was the door through which American workers were shoved into the neoliberal global labor market.
>
> By establishing the principle that U.S. corporations could

relocate production elsewhere and sell back into the United States, NAFTA undercut the bargaining power of American workers, which had driven the expansion of the middle class since the end of World War II. The result has been 20 years of stagnant wages and the upward
redistribution of income, wealth and political power.

NAFTA affected U.S. workers in four principal ways. First, it caused the loss of some 700,000 jobs as production moved to Mexico. Most of these losses came in California, Texas, Michigan, and other states where manufacturing is concentrated. To be sure, there were some job gains along the border in service and retail sectors resulting from increased trucking activity, but these gains are small in relation to the loses, and are in lower paying occupations. The vast majority of workers who lost jobs from NAFTA suffered a permanent loss of income.

Second, NAFTA strengthened the ability of U.S. employers to force workers to accept lower wages and benefits. As soon as NAFTA became law, corporate managers began telling their workers that their companies intended to move to Mexico unless the workers lowered the cost of their labor. In the midst of collective bargaining negotiations with unions, some companies would even start loading machinery into trucks that they said were bound for Mexico. The same threats were used to fight union organizing efforts. The message was: "If you vote in a union, we will move south of the border." With NAFTA, corporations also could more easily blackmail local governments into giving them tax reductions and other subsidies.

Third, the destructive effect of NAFTA on the Mexican agricultural and small business sectors dislocated several million Mexican workers and their families, and was a major cause in the dramatic increase in undocumented workers

> flowing into the U.S. labor market. This put further downward pressure on U.S. wages, especially in the already lower paying market for less skilled labor.
>
> Fourth, and ultimately most important, NAFTA was the template for rules of the emerging global economy, in which the benefits would flow to capital and the costs to labor. The U.S. governing class—in alliance with the financial elites of its trading partners—applied NAFTA's principles to the World Trade Organization, to the policies of the World Bank and IMF, and to the deal under which employers of China's huge supply of low-wage workers were allowed access to U.S. markets in exchange for allowing American multinational corporations the right to invest there....."[6]

Faux' main points are roughly true, but we can take it further. The American system of Alexander Hamilton, Henry Clay, and Abraham Lincoln was abandoned by the US without a thorough debate in the aftermath of the triumph of WWII in favor of Free Trade ideology, in part to ward off the perceived threat of Communism. The Baby Boom ended in 1962 which at a visceral level was evidence that the economy was weakening. Corporate America and Johnson could have used this clue to recognize the necessity of improving the economy so people would want to found a family, but instead they decided to outsource population growth. They liberalized immigration law in 1965 to bring in workers cheaper. We are now in a Free Trade intellectual environment and the capitalists are setting up an Extractive Plantation Capitalism environment increasing their margins by driving down wages.

We recognize Plantation Capitalism by following pattern:

1) Labor is sourced from wherever it is cheapest. On Barbados labor was initially cheapest from indentured servants, then the

masters invented chattel slavery and sourced labor from Africa. Today the jobs are moved to wherever the labor is cheapest or if the jobs can't be moved, cheap immigrant labor is brought in to disrupt the wage scale. Africa 250 years ago, Mexico today, China tomorrow, India next week.

2) Since labor is cheap, it is not valued highly and there is a psychological chasm between labor, ownership, and management. (Seems to be the case looking around the country).

3) Training of labor is minimal.

4) The market is not the workers. The less the workers consume the better.

5) It needs an external market (corollary to the above #4). It is not a complete system since it needs an external market. Right now the external market is the USA. This external market is being rapidly degraded by the Plantation Capitalism infestation in large part because the workers aren't paid enough and because a lot of workers aren't working.

6) There is a often a racial ethnic nature to Plantation Capitalism. When you are shopping the world for the cheapest workers, you will necessarily encounter diversity. If you are a Plantation Capitalist you will exploit this diversity to divide your workers up, brother against bubba against Julio so that in the end they all bow down to you, massa with moola. Also the more you can dehumanize your workers, the less you have to think about underpaying them.

6) It runs on fear and greed. There is often a militarized violent undertone. Since when did we need a Department of Homeland Security?

Unfortunately, the jobs created in Mexico fit our definition of Plantation Capitalism. In particular, they fit our definition of Extractive Plantation Capitalism because the profits generated by this exploitive practice are largely sent and spent outside Mexico. The market is not in the country (Mexico). That is a big part of why the Mexican economy has not benefited from

NAFTA driven exports. The jobs pay terribly. The profits are sent elsewhere, possibly to offshore corporate accounts. Plantation Capitalism isn't about community development.

5) This leads directly to our next point. As US wages are decreased due to job losses, intimidation of possible job losses, wage pressure from immigration, and lack of job creation, this decreases the size of the US market. This puts additional strain on US workers as their domestic market (employment demand to service the domestic economy) is further decreased in size because they have reduced income. Our government responds to this drop in wage demand by borrowing and printing money rather than fixing the problem.

Let's look again at the trade deficit budget deficit graph:

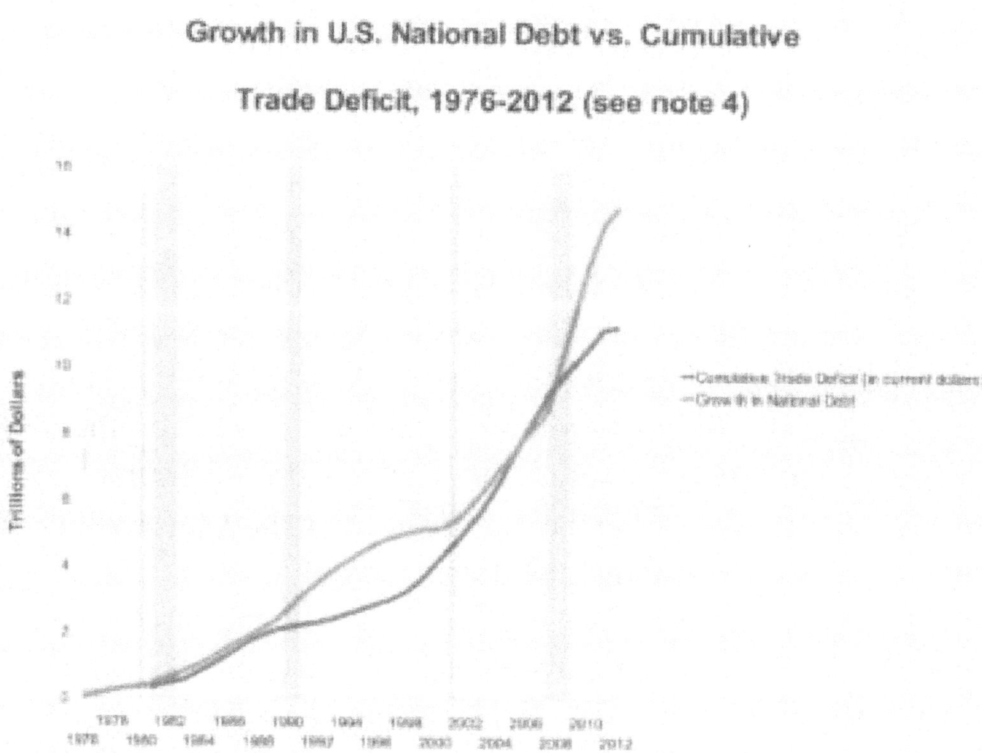

Notes:
1. Cumulative trade deficit expressed in current dollars.
2. Sources: U.S. Treasury (national debt);
Bureau of Economic Analysis (trade deficit)
3. U.S. National debt was $0.53 trillion in 1975. Chart above shows growth in the debt from that point, not the actual debt.
4. 2012 data through January.
5. Recessions shown in yellow bars.

England became impoverished paying for World War I and never really recovered its prewar status as a great power. The graph above suggests that we may be on a similar road to perdition. The external market for the Plantation Capitalism Economy is to some extent a credit card. This is not really sustainable. We had a 4 trillion dollar debt in 1994 when NAFTA became law and it has quadrupled since that time(18 trillion today). Our debt has entered La La land during the War on Terror and the Iraq war with a collapse in manufacturing. In contrast the North during the Civil War grew her manufacturing in a tremendous struggle and the nation emerged from the Civil War still on the road to greatness. If Abraham Lincoln had outsourced war production and let the bankers control his finances like George W. Bush the North would have lost the war and been in debilitating debt forever.

Total Manufacturing Jobs: (The following charts are from the Bureau of Labor Statistics.)

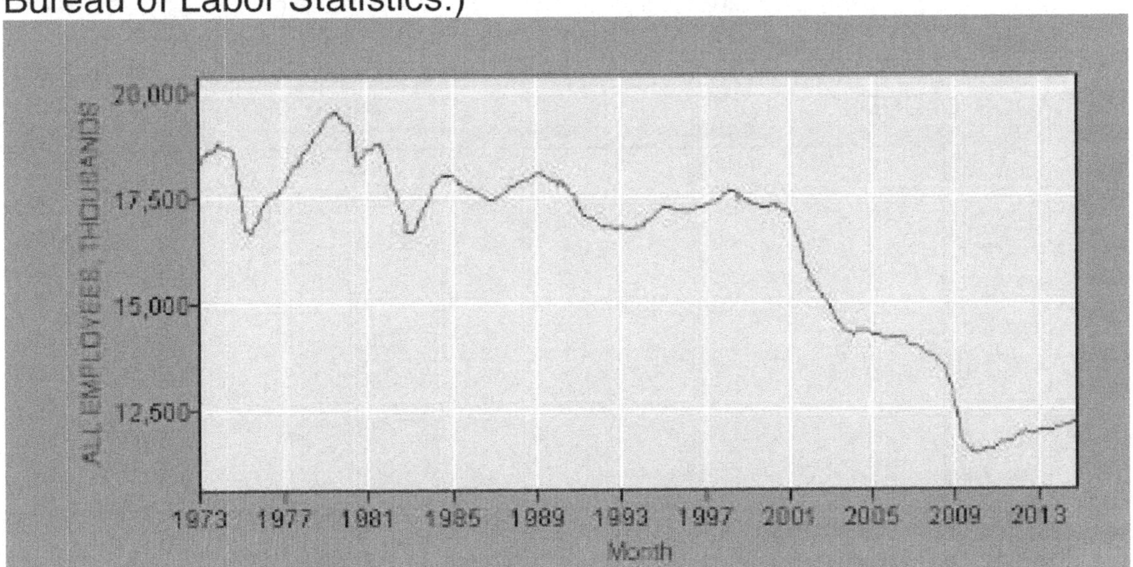

The graph above shows a decrease in American manufacturing workforce beginning with Paul Volcker raising interest rates during the Carter administration and then collapsing during the George W. Bush presidency. This is during a time of steady population growth with the Baby Boom generation in their prime working years. If you look at the curve from the Ford and Carter years (1976 -1979) manufacturing had in comparison a muted cyclical recovery in the economic boom of the 1990's (1993-1998) and then collapsed with the Bush presidency when the economy contracted.

Textile Mill Jobs:

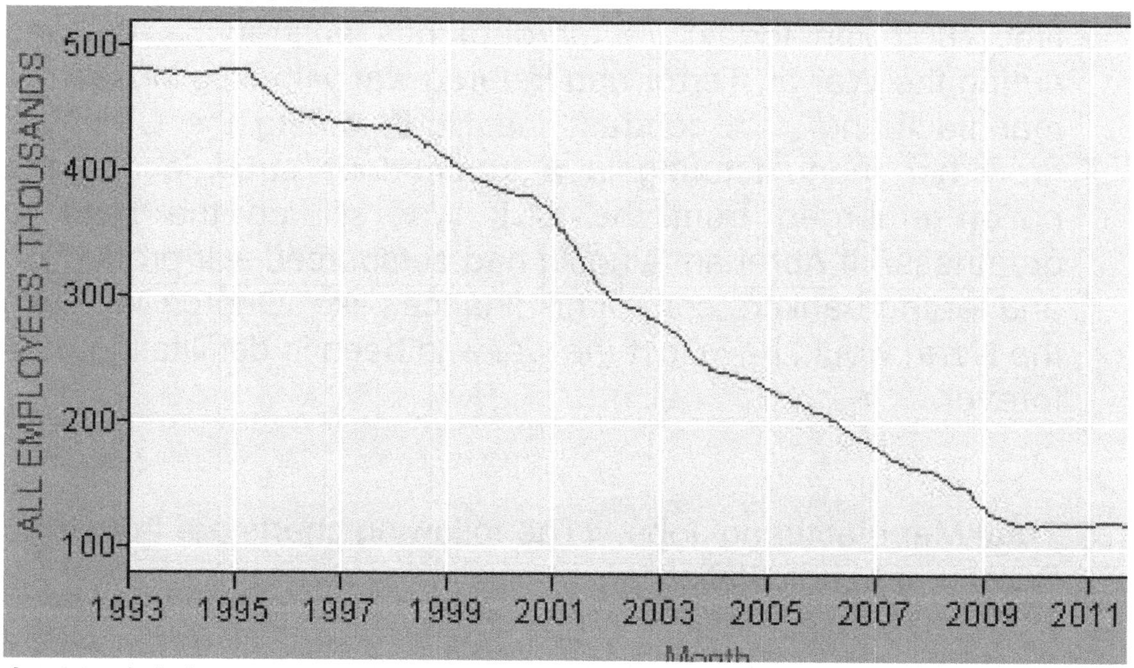

Apparel Jobs:

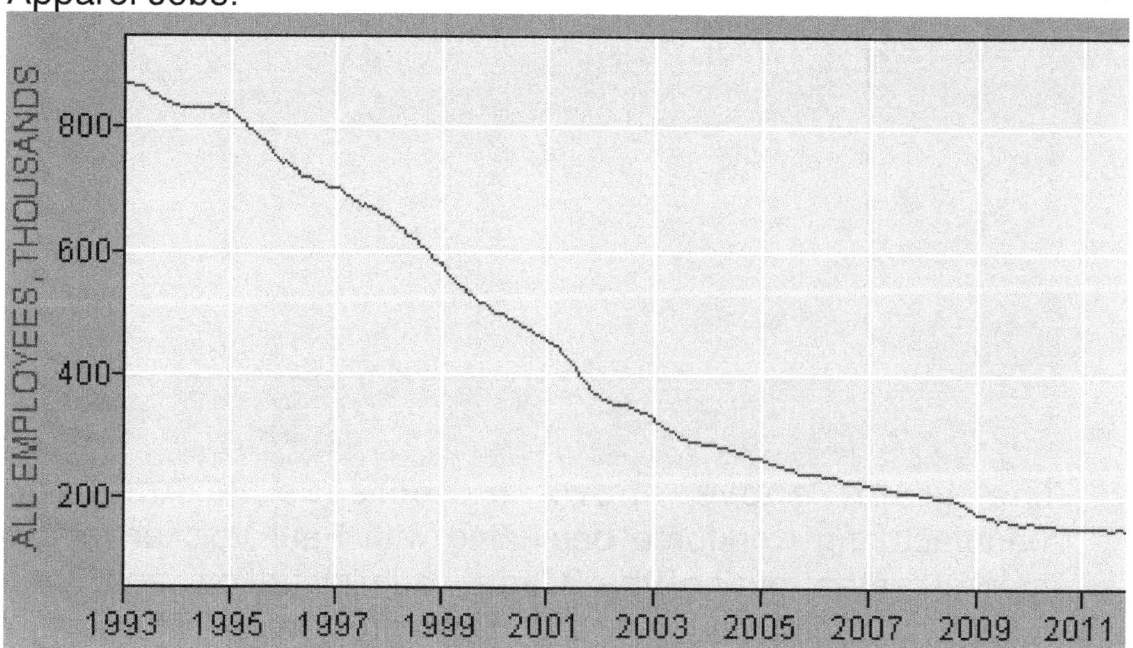

The textile and apparel workers were outsourced for no particular gain. These were easy jobs for the Plantation Capitalists to move so they took an early severe unremitting hit. This looks like a 330,000 textile job loss + 800,000 apparel job loss = 1,130,000 jobs in just these two categories alone. The employment numbers fall off a cliff starting with the passage of NAFTA. It is further likely that many of the jobs that are left are filled with cheap immigrant labor.

Food Manufacturing Jobs:

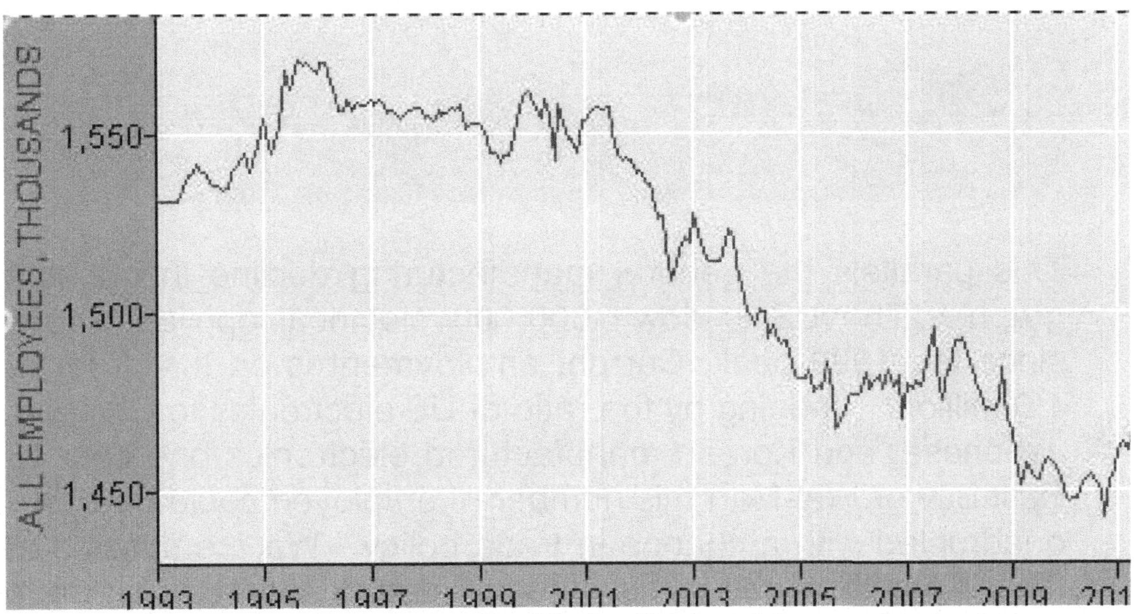

The United States is blessed with fertile land for agriculture. Geographically these jobs are to some extent fixed in the US (roughly analogous to petroleum jobs in Saudi Arabia). The wage scale in these jobs has been under severe pressure following NAFTA with mass immigration providing a source of cheap labor. Real wages in the meatpacking industry for example have fallen 45% from their peak.

Electrical Appliance Jobs:

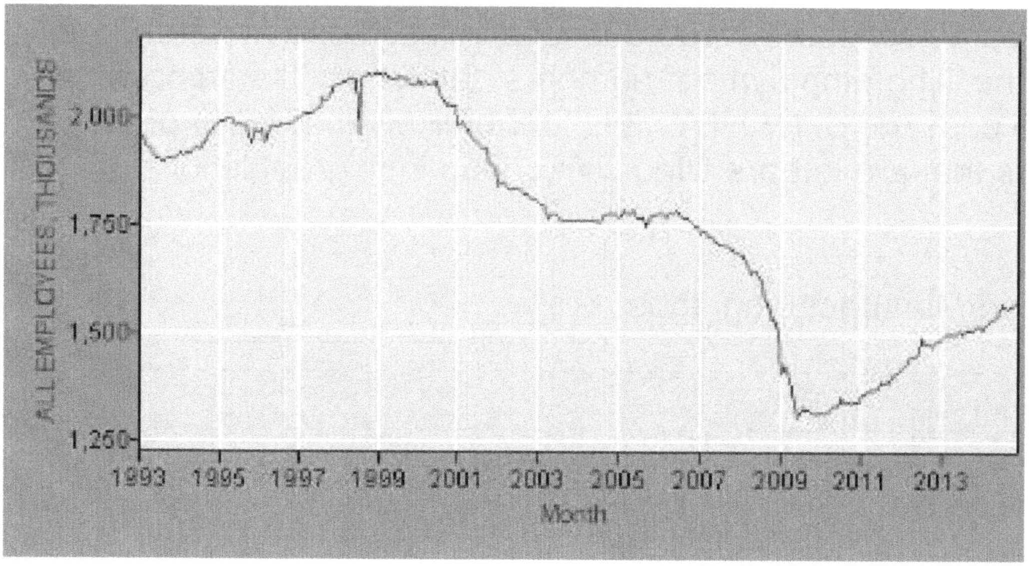

This parallels the general manufacturing decline in our first graph. The US is down 500,000 electrical appliance jobs since the 1999 peak. Current employment is on the order of 1.6 million. Judging by the ratio of US electronics to Chinese, Japanese, and Korean manufactured electronics one sees at Best Buy or Wal-Mart this number of employed could be easily quadrupled with a change in trade policy. We are missing at least 4.5 million jobs in this category due to poor/ corrupt trade policy.

Transportation Equipment Jobs:

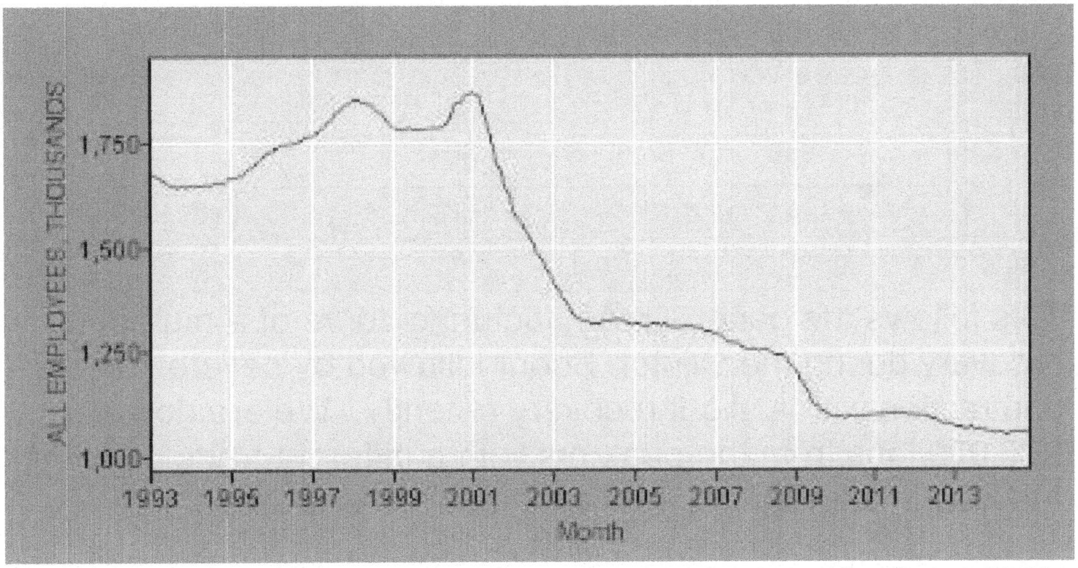

This parallels our general manufacturing curve in the 1990's but distressingly is showing absolutely no recovery unlike the electrical appliance curve above. When they say GM stands for gone to Mexico there is a reason. These have historically been very good jobs and ground zero for American manufacturing pride and central to being a great power. The curve above shows a loss of about 750,000 jobs. This could be dramatically improved with better policy. (Are our leaders taking the drugs they can't keep out of the country? Not an inspiring performance.)

Computers and Electronic Products Jobs:

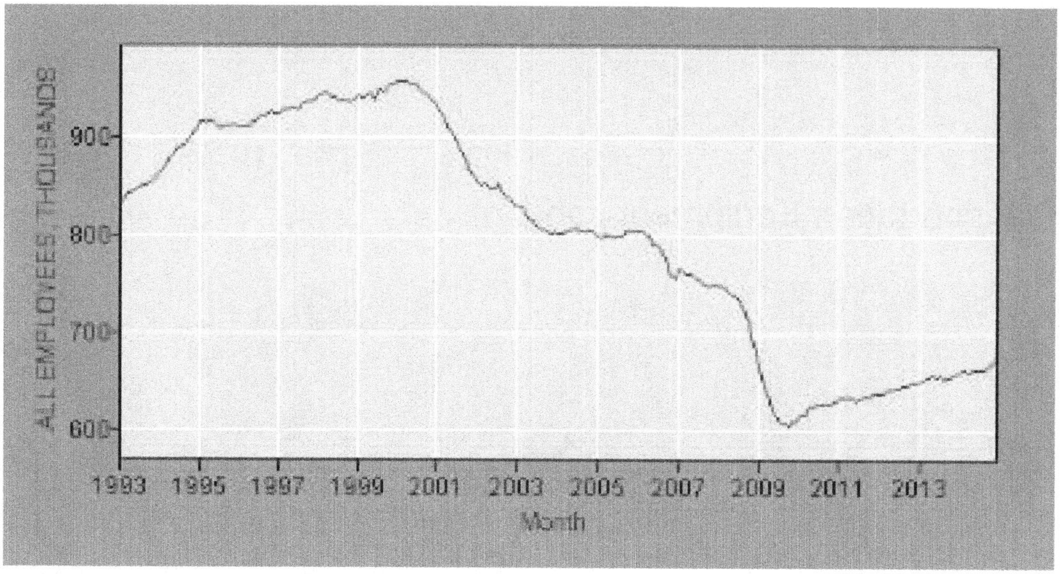

This follows the general manufacturing curve of a muted recovery during the Clinton Boom followed by severe contraction with a slight recovery recently. We are down 275,000 jobs from the peak but with a different trade policy the jobs in this sector could be increased dramatically.

Rubber and Plastics Jobs:

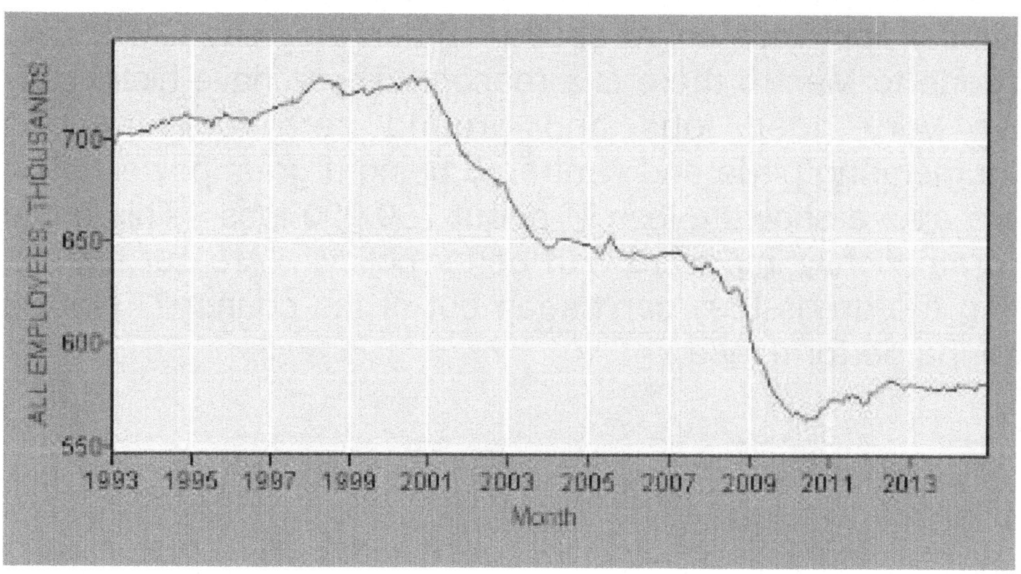

This follows the general manufacturing curve. It's not as bad as some of the others with a loss of 150,000 jobs (about 20%). Still, that's 150,000 families that are hurting.

Miscellaneous Manufacturing Jobs:

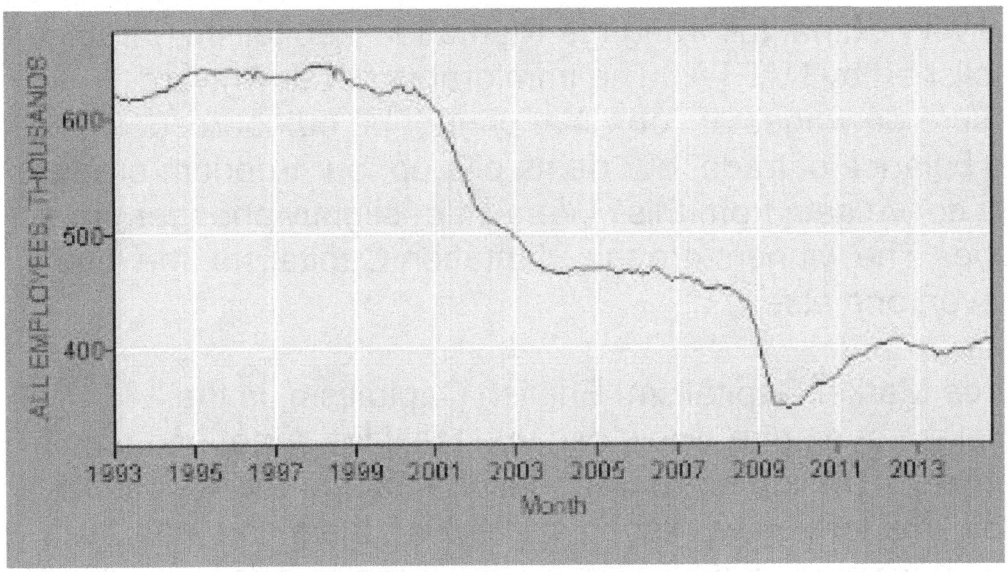

This is a sum of several small categories that are grouped together by the statisticians at the US Department of Labor, Bureau of Labor Statistics . It follows our general manufacturing curve and shows a loss of 200,000 jobs.

Furniture Manufacturing Jobs:

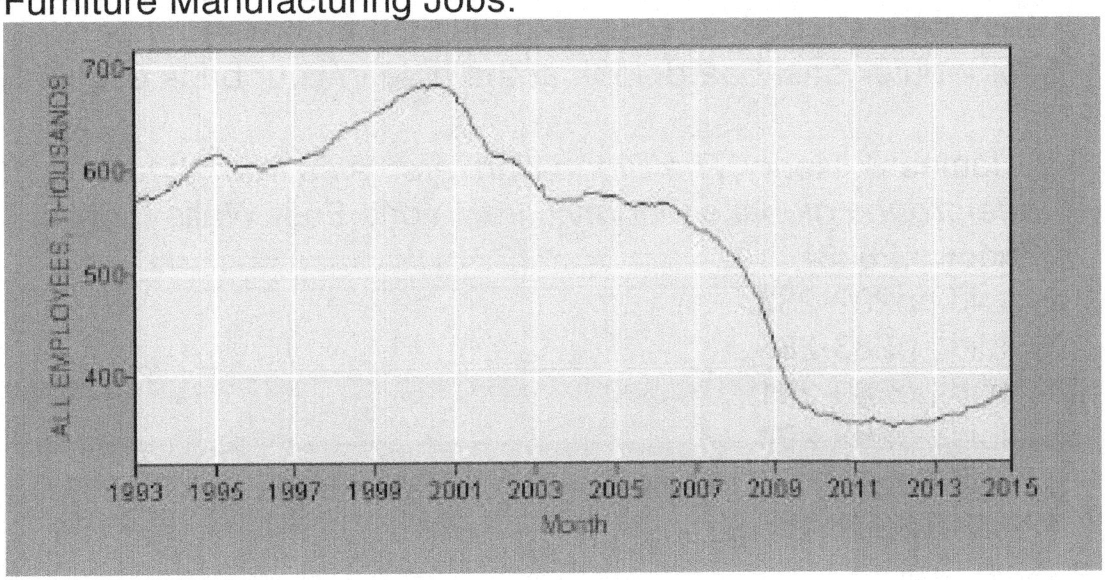

Again the same general curve with a peak to trough loss of 300,000 jobs.

Many, probably most, of these job losses are due to expanded trade with China, following the Plantation Capitalism paradigm established by NAFTA. The immigrants put downward pressure on wages of jobs that cannot be outsourced. There is no balance of trade, our debts pile up, our freedom erodes. What do we gain from this? Very little- slightly cheaper prices maybe. The winners are the Plantation Capitalists, the losers are everyone else.

Free Market Capitalism, English Capitalism, is the capitalism of empire. How can you tell if the American empire is for you? Do you run a transnational corporation producing goods in a foreign workshop and selling them in the US with an offshore bank account? If so, this empire is for you. If not, it's not. The empire has racked up 18.2 trillion dollars in debt. That's 56,000 per person, 127,000 per job, 254,000 per job good enough to produce revenue to pay off the debt. That doesn't count our unfunded liabilities of 100 trillion dollars when the baby boomers retire- multiply the above numbers by 5 for a quick dashboard look at the hole in your bank account.

1. James S. Henry, *The Blood Bankers: tales from the underground global economy* (New York: Four Walls Eight Windows,2003)
2. Ibid., p282-283.
3. Ibid., p283-285.
4. Ibid., p289-291.
5. Ibid., p293-294.
6. Jeff Faux, "NAFTA's impact on US Workers", 12/9/2013(EPI Blog)

Cui Bono?

Who wins?

The question of who wins with globalization is not sufficiently discussed. Let's study it briefly.

Vestey Capitalism

"It's not what you make, it's what you keep."

William and Edmund Vestey were two sons of a provisions broker. They grew up in Liverpool in the late Victorian Period. In 1876, the 17 year old William was sent by his father to see if there were any products in Chicago that they might sell. When William visited the Chicago slaughterhouses, he noticed that the best cuts were processed and the rest was thrown out. This struck him as a waste of perfectly good food. William set up a business where he bought the trimmings cheap, canned them, and shipped the corned beef back to Liverpool. He had enough money to retire by thirty.

Which he hated. He hated not working. He hated spending money he wasn't earning. "I never spend any of my profits. I save every farthing. I live on what I earned twenty years ago."[1] William enjoyed telling recruits that when he was making 20,000 pounds per year, he, his wife, and four children lived off of 500 pounds and saved the rest.

He went back to work. William traveled to Argentina. There was a surplus of beef. The Argentinians would kill a cow for the hide and let the carcass rot. There were plentiful pigeons but the Argentinians didn't eat them. He had the local freezing works, La Negra, pack and freeze a shipment of pigeons and ship them back to Liverpool. The trial run was a success. Soon this necessitated building a cold storage facility in Liverpool. The need for cold storage was great and their business expanded and they built additional cold storage capacity.

They soon recognized that the English appetite for meat was not met locally and that with refrigerated ships and cold storage they could import food from around the world and sell it locally. They imported eggs from China, beef from Argentina, poultry from Russia, sheep from New Zealand and Australia. They were vertically integrated with their own packing houses, ships, and cold storage. Profits exploded. By 1914 William and Edmund had each made £10 million (one billion pounds in todays money or roughly 1.5 billion dollars each).

In 1914, of course, the WWI came. The British and Allied armies needed food. The Vestey brothers built cold storage facilities at Boulogne, Le Havre, and Dunkirk. In 1914 the Vesteys had cold storage in Britain, Russia, China and seven ships (four of which were refrigerated). In 1919 the brothers had ranches, packing houses, and cold storage in Australia, New Zealand, South Africa, Madagascar, France, Spain, Portugal, and 12 ships. The war was clearly expansionary for them.

The war was also expansionary for the government. Until 1914, if a British company made money abroad it was not taxed on it unless it brought the money back to England. The

1914 Finance Act, passed to meet the wartime needs for revenue, changed the rules of the game. British companies were taxed on profits whether they brought them home or not. The Vesteys considered this grossly unfair because their principal competitor, the American Beef Trust, paid no taxes in England because it was a foreign company. Unless it sent the profits on its British operations back to the US, it didn't pay taxes there either.

William added up the tax bite using a worst case scenario. On a £100 profit, they would first have to pay an excess profits tax of 40%. Of the £60 remaining, income tax and super tax would take £31.5 leaving £28.5. If they had to pay inheritance tax at 40%, this would leave them with only £17.1. They considered this over the top so they went to see the President of the Board of Trade, Sir John Bradbury. Treasury could not budge because to exempt one company would lead in the end to exempt them all. In this exchange a Treasury official told them that taxation would not stop them from earning money- their real central point of contention was that their rivals could keep more than they could. This was a Eureka moment for them. It was no longer about what they could make, it was about what they could keep. High taxes were here to stay.

The brothers ingeniously set about making an offshore empire, or rather, making sure that the profits from their offshore empire did not become absorbed by British taxes. They traveled to Chicago in 1915 and consulted an American lawyer. He said, "What's the matter with you people? You are the third Englishman I've had in here this week on this same business."[2] Their plan broke out the international part of their business which they assigned to an American company, National Cold Storage of New York, and the English part of their business, Union Cold Storage. They then tried to move as much of the profits from the British part of the business (Union) to the international part of the business (National). They were overaggressive on this and the British tax authorities did not allow many of the deductions they were claiming. However, on the central issue they were able to move the international part of their business out of the reach of the British tax authorities. Basically everything that was not physically in Britain was beyond the taxman.

Furthermore they moved to Argentina which had no income tax.

Still, at some level the Vesteys felt that England was their home and longed to return- they just didn't want to pay high taxes. On February 22, 1919 William sent the following letter to the Prime Minister, Lloyd George.

> "The object of this letter is to set before you the impossible position in which our purely English firm of Vestey Brothers is placed owing to the freedom from taxation given to the American Beef Trust on practically the whole of their business in England, while we should have to pay almost the whole of any income we might derive from the business, and as the Revenue officials have already been discussing for 15 years the question of taxation of the American Beef Trust, to ask if equality of treatment cannot be given to us now while we are alive."

William showed the tax calculation that they would get taxed 92 % if they followed the rules where as the American Beef Trust paid no tax on 90% of their business and only a small amount on the remaining 10%. The letter continues ...

> "We are told that the government would like to get England out of the clutches of the American Beef Trust

> but in fact the Trust themselves could never have conceived so perfect and simple a device for consolidating and extending their practical monopoly of the frozen meat trade as that the British Government should exempt them from taxation and impose a tax of 92 % on the profits of any British firms which have the temerity to oppose them. It appears impossible but that is the present position."

William said if he could be taxed like the American Beef Trust, he would return the company to England.

> "The government will not lose any revenue by allowing us to return; they are not receiving any now and never can under the above conditions, whereas if we return they will receive many thousands of pounds annually from business we shall do in England, in addition to the death duties we must pay and sums they will lose if we are domiciled abroad. Further, should we be permitted to return, we shall find work for 3,000 to 5,000 Englishmen, instead of that number of foreigners abroad. We ask for no preference, advantage, or assistance in any way, merely an equal chance in our own country, and it does seem to me that an Englishman who only wants to work, should have to petition for equality of treatment with a foreigner, is a most pitiable thing."[3]

Lloyd George suggested that William should take his case to the Royal Commission on Income Tax. On 7/31/1919 William gave testimony to the commission which has broad implications for globalization. He wanted income made abroad to be tax free. "If I kill a beast in the Argentine and sell the product in Spain, this country can get no tax on that business. You may do what you like, but you cannot have it."

Commissioner: You would not object to be assessed on your foreign profits which you sent over to this country?

William Vestey: The net result would be that none whatsoever would be sent over.

Commissioner: I suppose you would not object to this: assessment on your business excluding the trading between foreign companies?

William Vestey: In a business of this nature you cannot say how much is made in one country and how much is made in another. You kill an animal and the product of that animal is sold in 50 different countries. You cannot say how much is made in England and how much is abroad.

Commissioner: Where are you domiciled at present? In this country?

William Vestey: No, Buenos Aires. I am technically abroad at present, but I came over here specially to appear before this Commission. The present position of affaires suits me admirably. I am abroad; I pay nothing. I am talking against my own interest, but I was born in the good old town of Liverpool and I want to die in this country, and I want to come and work here; that is why I am here. Really I am doing myself harm by making all these propositions. If I have got to live abroad I am speaking against myself.

The conversation turned to the income tax. Did Sir William realize it was a tax on individual income. William said that he did, but thought it would be covered under the profit tax.

Commissioner: No, you would still have to pay it because you are a resident here. Are you not to pay anything for the advantage of living here?

William Vestey: (Silence)

Commissioner: With respect, I should like to have an answer. It is one that has agitated me a good deal since the witness has been in the chair.

Chairman: Sir William is going to give an answer. I think he was indicating it by gesture. You are prepared, of course, to pay income tax as a resident upon your income, are you not? - Yes, I think I must say so.[4]

The Vesteys began to realize that they were not going to get their needs met by negotiating with the tax authorities, so they set about solving their problem themselves. They set up an offshore trust.

They directed a revenue stream from their business, Union International Company Limited to a Paris trust set up for their heirs. This used standard tax avoidance strategy of the wealthy. However, in routine trusts the individual setting up the trust is not allowed to benefit personally from the trust. Their solution was to have the trust have wide power of investment to be carried out at the direction of "certain authorized persons" - the Vestey brothers themselves. Here is how it went down. The Paris trustees sent money listed as "unsecured loans and advances" to the Western United Investment Company in Britain, a Vestey holding company. Western acted as a personal banker to the Vesteys loaning them money to pay their living expenses. Since it was listed as a loan rather than income, no tax.

Several notes on the Vesteys.

1) They made money, a lot of money, by working hard and recognizing opportunities and taking them.

2) They made the lives of the English better by bringing them meat and eggs at a reasonable price. Having access to eggs all year round so you can bake cakes and breads that rise is a definite improvement in living standards. Being able to eat

meat when you have the notion is better than a diet of potatoes and cabbage.

3) The issues that confronted the Vesteys are central to a globalized economy. Other companies may not talk it out with the Prime Minister and the Royal Commission on Income Tax, but they are unavoidably thinking of the same issues. Witness that the Vesteys were third English company to meet with the Chicago lawyer the week they began proceedings to move the nonBritish part of their empire out of the reach of the English taxes. All major international companies are tuned into "It's not what you make, it's what you keep."

Their attitudes may seem self serving, and certainly seemed self serving to the English government who had endured a horrific war, but they spring from human nature and are closer to how people will actually behave given the chance than we might want to imagine. Trading companies that are ostensibly located in country A but are making money moving products between countries B and C will chafe at taxes from their home country. They will try to find ways around those taxes. This is a weakness of Anglo Saxon capitalism - you may source from the world but you do not have the loyalty of the world, you scarcely have loyalty from the companies whose sea lanes you protect. When Sir William says, "If I kill a beast in the Argentine and sell the product in Spain, this country can get no tax on that business. You may do what you like, but you cannot have it.", he is to some extent stating the facts of the case. People who are as smart as the Vesteys, who have worked as hard as the Vesteys, will have a tendency to want to keep their money and will not arrange their affairs to give the taxman a good hard shot at their stash if they can avoid it. In globalized business you can often assign the profits to your offshore subsidiary in the lowest possible tax jurisdiction.

Vestey also had a point that the tax men should have paid attention to. It was wrong for Vestey to be punitively taxed and for the Americans to have the same access to the British market that Vestey did. It is true the billionaire in today's money didn't make a sympathetic figure because of his success, but his principal was correct. The home team companies should not be penalized when serving their home market. Again, this is where a tariff or sales tax instead of a tax on profits would be of utility. Consumption taxes could extract money from the beef trade, but they would not unfairly penalize British beef producers compared with American or other foreign producers.

The Tax Viewpoint.

"We don't pay taxes. Only the little people pay taxes."

-Leona Helmsley

Let's look at sources of federal revenue in the period 1950 - 2012.

Revenue from corporate income taxes was 5 -6 % GDP in the early 1950's and fell to 1.3% GDP in 2010. There was a slight drop in the corporate income tax rate of from 50% to 35% but this does not account for the 3/4 drop in corporate revenue! What is happening? Well either corporate profitability has dropped relative to GDP or the corporations are finding ways to evade taxes. The chart below of corporate profits as a percentage of GDP shows that corporate profits did drop in 1981 when Volcker raised interest rates to stop inflation but since have rebounded nicely; however, tax revenue has not. As the above story of the Vesteys shows, globalization makes it easy to evade taxes by not showing a profit in the business entity that the tax man has jurisdiction over.

Figure 1. Sources of Federal Tax Revenue, Fiscal Year 2010

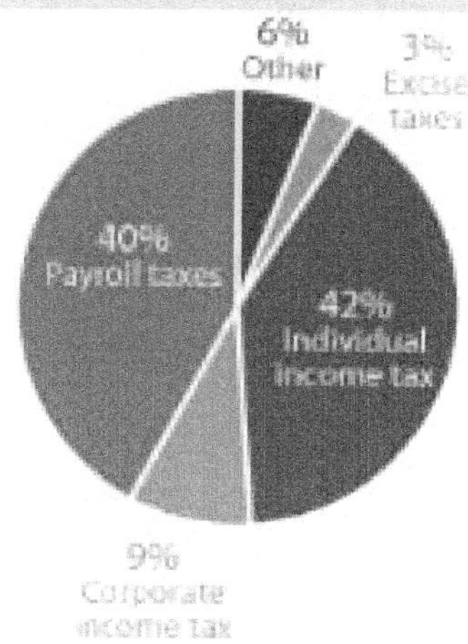

Source: Budget of the United States Government, Fiscal Year 2012, Historical Tables Table 2.1; http://www.whitehouse.gov/omb/budget/Historicals

Just 9 % Federal Revenue from corporate tax; in 1950 it paid 26%.

Figure 2. Sources of Federal Revenue, Fiscal 1950-2010

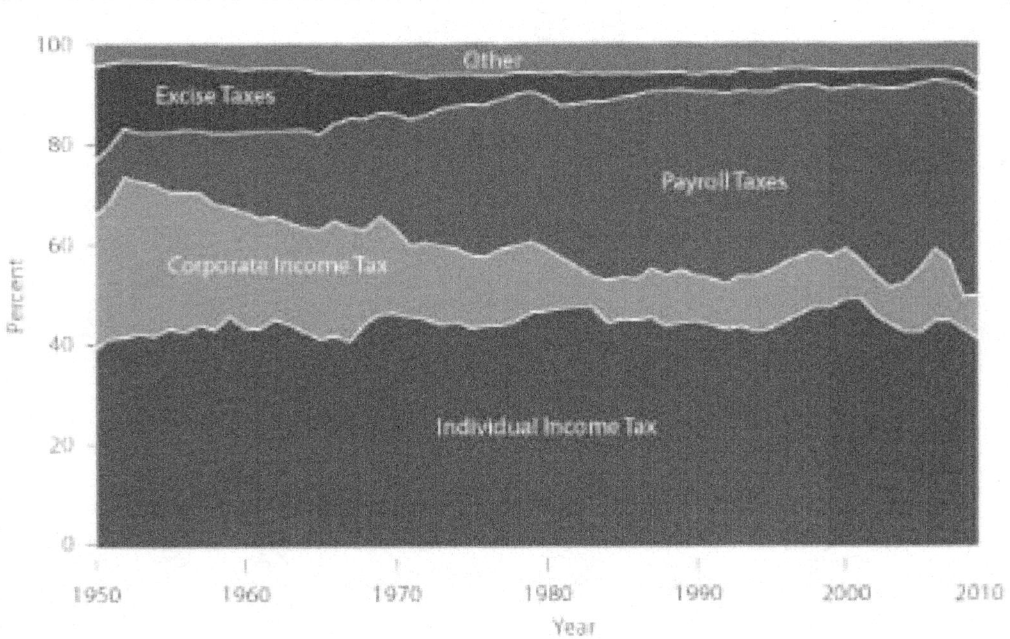

Source: Budget of the United States Government, Fiscal Year 2012, Historical Tables: Table 2.1; http://www.whitehouse.gov/omb/budget/Historicals

The above chart shows the corporate and excise taxes (tariffs on foreigners) decreasing with the tax burden dumped on the shoulders of the middle class in the form of higher payroll taxes. The revenue from corporate taxes could easily be doubled if globalization was restructured to benefit the workers.

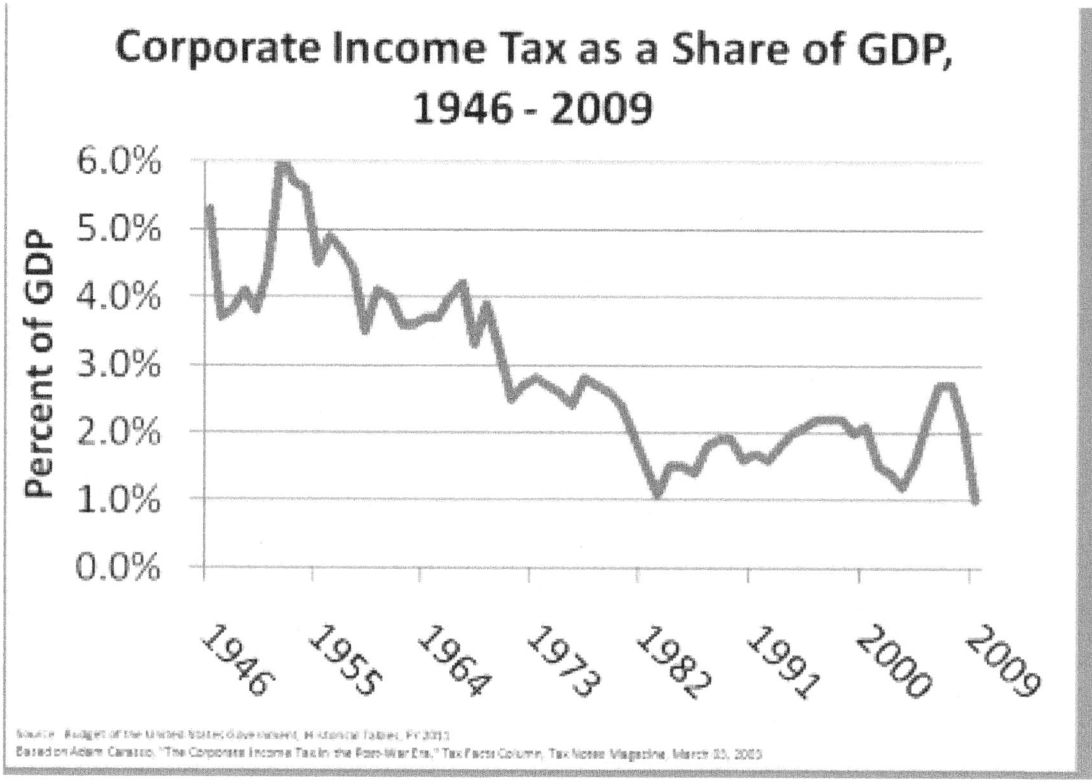

The above charts show is that the government take from excise taxes and corporate taxes has been dramatically reduced since 1950. This burden has fallen on the workers in an increased payroll and medicare tax. We are to a large extent dealing with (or actually not dealing with) "Dark Money" (think "Dark Matter") that is not showing up on the main corporate balance sheet. When corporate insiders make a habit of evading the government tax man, it is likely that the minority shareholder's interests are not being looked after in a straightforward moral way. (Would you want to be a minority shareholder with the Vesteys?)

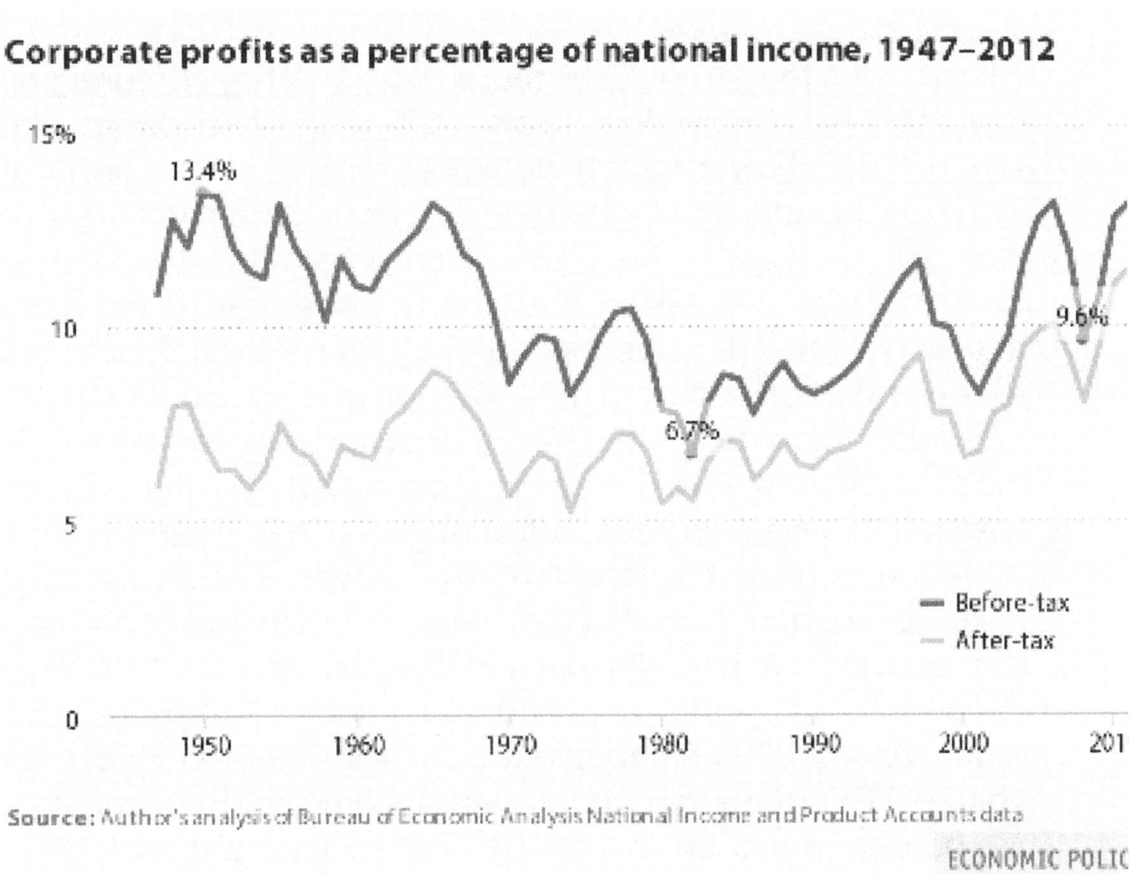

The above chart shows that the after tax percentage of corporate profits vs the national income has gone from 6-7% in the 1950's to 11 % in the supposedly progressive Obama administration. (i.e. the corporations are keeping 4% of GDP that Eisenhower would have made them pay to balance the books, but Obama is borrowing. If the GDP is 17.3 trillion and corporations are keeping 4% of it = .04 x 17 trillion = 680 billion dollars that has gone missing.) This is a consequence of globalization and the reduction of tax rates from 50% to 35 %. In 1950 the corporate tax paid for approximately 26% of federal revenue, now it pays for 9%. It's clear from this that the corporations have been large tax beneficiaries of globalization above and beyond the ability to practice

Plantation Capitalism by oppressing labor externally and selling to the US market.

If we collected 2% of GDP more in taxes from corporations today (still well below the rate that was done during the Truman / Eisenhower years) we would receive on the order of 374 billion in additional revenue or about 2,634 dollars per employed American. The Federal corporate tax revenue in fiscal 2015 was 341 billion, the charts above make the case that if with a few adjustments we could more than double the rate revenue received from corporations and we would still not be back at the rate of revenue extraction maintained in the 1950's. This tax avoidance is connected at the hip to globalization. Another loss to the taxpayer has been the loss of revenue from all the jobs that aren't here. At an effective tax rate of roughly 32% (income tax 16.7 % + medicare and social security 15.3 %) the loss of 3.4 million jobs to China, 896,000 jobs to Japan, and 800,000 + jobs to Mexico = 5.1 million jobs x 36,000 salary/job x 32% = 58.7 billion in lost tax revenue. This does not count state income and sales taxes. This burden must be borne by those who are still lucky enough to have a job. (About 413 dollars per employed worker in the country). Adding these lost revenues together:
2,634 + 413 = 3047 dollars per job that we could give back to each taxpayer if we were less globalized.

Additional losses accrue to the taxpayer from the low salaries that have been present since 1973. If salaries had had simply a modest increase since 1973 of 50% adjusted for inflation (.8%/ year), the tax revenue would increase by about 50% and this would add roughly a trillion dollars per year to the national tax revenue (i.e. there would be no budget deficit).

If our economy had been healthier, it is possible that much of the social spending that is directed to the criminal justice system and welfare system could be avoided with better jobs. (39 billion spent on prisons each year which is far higher than most countries). If the Plantation Capitalists were not putting Miracle Gro on our geopolitical rivals it is possible we could have more of a peace dividend and cut the Department of Defense by 150 - 200 billion dollars but in the present circumstances that is probably not wise. (Another 1000 dollars per taxpayer per year for the road not taken.)

Clearly, from a fiscal standpoint, globalization is a disaster with the rich and powerful avoiding taxes and the middle class loaded with burdens that in truth can no longer be borne.

The Consumer.

One beneficiary of globalization is the consumer, who gains from falling prices and increased competition of providers of goods and services. This division of labor is less important with a continent wide country such as the United States where there is significant domestic competition, than it would be for a small country such as Switzerland. Still, there is a definite increase in purchasing power. If the consumer is also a worker, the benefits can be roughly estimated by inflation adjusted wages. Inflation adjusted wages for a male worker peaked in 1973 in the US and have flatlined since that time with a slow drop off of about 10% using official inflation statistics which probably understate the decline. So if the consumer is consuming wages he is losing slowly- or actually rather rapidly - because in the 24 years before 1973 (when globalization was a much smaller part of the economy) wages doubled. If with enlightened leadership wages, had continued to increase at the same rate of 3 % per year wages, should have tripled in the 40 years since 1973. Certainly with the technology improvements we have had in the last 50 years we should have had wages go up 1% per year and that would have resulted in a 60% increase in purchasing power.

We need to be open to new ideas from around the globe but not let Plantation Capitalists oppress our workers. For instance, letting Honda make cars in the United States for the US market is not an assault on our wage scale, but if they source autos from Mexico at 2.50 per hour wage and take the profit back to Japan we should put obstacles in their path. There are ways we can have the good ideas of the world and the benefits of competition brought home to our consumer, but we cannot let this undermine our wage scale.

As outlined in the chapter on mathematical modeling, the growth of debt public debt is strongly connected to the trade deficit. This public debt in turn is associated with a general debasement of the dollar. Thus we have had slow and gradual inflation in the last 50 years when the free trade theorist would tell you that free trade was holding down prices. This is in clear contrast to Henry Clay's speech in 1832 on the American System when he showed that prices in a relatively closed economy were gradually dropping. This was the general pattern of prices of manufactured goods in the 19th century with the exception of the greenback period of the Civil War. So to leave a free trade economy might in the short run lead to higher prices, however in the longer run, there will be greater price stability than we currently enjoy because we won't have a constant monetary inflation.

This monetary inflation will continue as long as Plantation Capitalists are sourcing from elsewhere where the low wages are and shipping product to the US. As long as they are following this business plan we will run a trade deficit. As long we run a trade deficit the politicians will keep spending money they don't have to promote temporary stability which will cause a continuous inflation.

The Bankers and Financiers

The bankers have been huge winners in the globalized economy at several levels. From 1970 to 2003 over 3 trillion dollars were loaned by the West to developing countries. There has been a tremendous amount of corruption associated with these transactions with third world elites raking off large amounts of this money and stashing it in off shore banking accounts.

Joseph Mobutu, a former officer in the Belgian army seized power in Zaire (formerly the Belgian Congo) in 1960 in a CIA backed coup. By 1980 Zaire had Africa's largest foreign debt at 5 billion dollars. Most of his extravagant plans for development produced little in the way of positive results. The Inga Shaba power plant ran a 1700 mile transmission line (the world's longest) from the mouth of the Congo river to Shaba province where the copper was. It never used more than 1/5 of its capacity. The original estimated cost was 275 million dollars but when the corrupt payouts were over it cost 1.2 billion. When copper prices crashed, Zaire (Congo) was stuck with a huge un-payable debt.

When Mobutu was deposed in 1997, his fortune was estimated at greater than 4 billion dollars. He had mansions in Switzerland, Morocco, South Africa, France, Belgium, Spain, Portugal, and three palaces in Zaire. The wine collection in his Portuguese castle was worth 2.3 million. He had 500 double decker buses, a fleet of jumbo jets, and a supermarket. The bankers got to stash his cash. The people of the Congo (Zaire) got a ridiculous bill.[5]

This pattern of the Third World elite taking out a credit card on their country's wealth, transferring 50 % of the money to their private offshore accounts, and then dumping the debt on their citizens has been repeated over and over.

The banks make a lot of money financing the drug trade. The Mexican drug trade is estimated at between 13 - 49 billion a year. In 2012 HSBC was fined 1.9 billion for laundering 881 million in drug trafficking. " HSBC is being held accountable for stunning failures of oversight - and worse, that led the bank to permit narcotics traffickers and others to launder hundreds of millions of dollars through HSBC subsidiaries and facilitate hundreds of millions more in transactions with sanctioned countries," said Lanny Breuer, assistant attorney general. Unfortunately, the bank managed to avoid being criminally prosecuted so the above sanction will probably just be seen as the cost of doing business. HSBC's share price rose 2.8 p to 644 p the day of the fine.

According to the US Senate the bank had a "pervasively polluted" culture for many years. HSBC moved billions around the financial system for Mexican drug lords, terrorists, and governments on sanctions list. HSBC's Mexican operations moved 7 billion into US operations which the Senate was told was tied to drug money.

The primary method used by Columbian narcotics traffickers to launder their money is the Black Market Peso Exchange (BMPE). The drug lords use the proceeds from selling cocaine to buy goods in the US. These goods are then shipped to Columbia and sold to obtain pesos, and the laundered pesos are then used to finance their criminal activities. This is obviously facilitated by "free trade".

In 1989 John Williamson codified the "Washington Consensus", ten broadly accepted policy recommendations which were and are part of the groupthink of the International

Monetary Fund, World Bank, and US Treasury Department which were believed to be necessary for the recoveries of countries in Latin America from the economic crises of the 1980's. These 10 points were:

1. Fiscal policy discipline with avoidance of large fiscal deficits relative to GDP.
2. Redirection of public spending from subsidies to education, healthcare, and infrastructure investment.
3. Tax reform- broadening the tax base and adopting moderate tax rates.
4. Interest rates that are market determined and positive in real terms.
5. Competitive exchange rates.
6. Trade liberalization.
7. Liberalization of foreign direct investment.
8. Privatization of state enterprises.
9. Deregulation; abolition of regulations that impede market entry or restrict competition.
10. Legal security for property rights.

1. The first of these is in general prudent (it would be better if we had policies that allowed us not to run large deficits on a chronic basis as well - but if we took our own medicine at this point the economy would collapse).
2. When you are cutting the budget healthcare and education often get in the crossfire. Infrastructure spending, on the other hand, often is connected at the hip with massive corruption in the Third World - See Mr Mobutu above. However, as above, the banks tend to get paid on these projects. There is of course a tremendous need for infrastructure in the developing world, but the benefits of these projects tend to flow upwards.
3. Tax reform done well can be beneficial. It's not always easy to implement satisfactory policy because the lawmakers may respond to incentives that may not be in the best interest of the citizens.

4. One of the hallmarks of Third World countries is wide unstable swings in interest rates. When they are unstable and not meeting the need of your country that is evidence of failure to produce a stable internal milieu in your country.
5. How you set your exchange rates can influence trade flows - see Lamprey Capitalism. What is good for one country may be (likely is) unfair to another.
6. Trade liberalization - this makes it impossible for developing countries to protect their domestic market. (Actually, looking at the shelves of Wal Mart or Best Buy, it is difficult for developed countries to protect their market with trade liberalization without a plan to protect their markets. It's a tautology- if you don't protect your market, it's not protected.) It allows developed countries to colonize less developed countries. Note the lack of development in sub Saharan Africa and Latin America which complied with this nonsense with the dramatic growth of China, Korea, and Japan which did not comply. For that matter, in the nineteenth century the US and Germany had large tariffs and refused to be colonized by Great Britain.
Note that Third World countries with oil wealth (Venezeula), copper wealth (Chile), etc may have difficulty producing a diversified economy because the cost of labor will make other businesses uncompetitive with their competitors. Again, building a cell membrane/wall around the economy with tariffs is a way a country may develop into a diversified economy. This is also important at a human level because people may find their true calling in a field outside of what their countries competitive advantage would have them go into.
7. Liberalization of foreign direct investment - this allows businesses with connections to international money - banks - to pick up valuable assets for pennies on the dollar when a financial storm strikes or is engineered. This benefits

foreign finance and native elites.

Worse for the Third World, the close financial ties of the Third World elite and the Banking Elite lead to massive capital outflow in times of financial crisis contributing mightily to the instability of Third World capital.

8. Privatization of state enterprises. Cutting back on a bloated bureaucracy sounds good in theory and would be good in fact provided the public interest is properly looked after. The Homestead act was a great move in the right direction. Unfortunately when powerful moneyed interests get to prey on the people's assets the results can look less charming. The privatization of Russian mineral wealth in the Yeltsin era was largely a rip off of the Russian people by borderline criminal and criminal business entities. The oil wealth in Nigeria similarly goes to the political elite and the oil companies rather than the people who live in the area of the oil.

9. Deregulation; abolition of regulations that impede market entry or restrict competition. Again, this makes it difficult to protect your people and their jobs. The displacement of about 2 million Mexican farmers was a result of this kind of thinking and led to massive immigration, child hunger, and decreased wages in Mexico and the US as the displaced sought work elsewhere. Countries like China that have insisted on trade terms that meet their national priorities have done much better than countries that have followed this prescription.

This philosophy leads quickly to Plantation Capitalists making the rules that should be within the purview of government. The neoliberal agenda above displacing 2 million Mexican farmers and dumping them as illegal immigrants in the US has parallels with Mrs Gerard destroying the village of Ballinglass to make way for her cows, Lord Palmerston depopulating his Irish estates and dumping the population on Canada with a mortality that rivaled the middle passage, and the Duchess of Sutherland during the Highland clearances expropriating the land formerly held in common and dumping the population in America.

It should not be forgotten that "free market" Plantation Capitalists were able to buy slaves very cheap. So cheap, in fact they were able to mistreat them in the West Indies to the point that they died faster than they had children (a concentration camp version of slavery). It made good financial sense to use them up rather than to treat them right. 260,000 slaves were imported into the English West Indies between 1640 and 1700 but only 100,000 were alive in 1700.[6] Modern day Plantation Capitalists are using various techniques to drive down wages such as destroying peasant farming communities and using the displaced near starving masses to constitute a desperate proletariat to drive down salaries in the Third World and through immigration and Free Trade the developed world. Having minimum standards of pay and worker safety as a condition to be in a trading block would help stop this race to the bottom much as ending slavery improved the bargaining position of workers every where. It should also be noted that real sustained wealth was not created by abusing people like this but in communities where work was more valued (today Massachusetts is richer than Jamaica, although in 1713 Jamaica was the wealthiest and most important colony in the British Empire).

10. Legal Security for property rights. Property rights are important. However, people are important too and many of the deals that have been done in the Third World have been done under duress. This is an area for negotiation to make sure the different parties involved come to a fruitful compromise.

Digression on Chile.

Chile has an interesting history economic history with several experiments run by different central planners with less than fantastic results.

1970 Dr. Salvador Allende won the presidency with a plurality of 36.9 % of the votes; since it was only a plurality the election was placed in the hands of the Chilean congress which after some delay appointed Allende who assumed office 11/3/1970.

Allende began implementing *La via chilena al socialism* ("the Chilean Path to Socialism). The plan called for nationalization of copper mining, banking, health care, education, free milk for children. It called for seizure and redistribution of land (this program had already been started by his predecessor Eduardo Frei Montalva). All estates greater than 80 hectares (197 acres) were seized and redistributed. The plan also called for increasing employment in the nationalized industries and in public works programs.

The socialist Allende spent heavily in health, education, and welfare. The National Supplementary Food Program was extended to all pregnant women and primary school children.

Malnutrition in children under age 6 fell 17%. Bread prices were fixed. State programs distributed food to the hungry; state involvement in grocery distribution reached 33%. 3000 scholarships were given to Mapuches Indian children. From 1971 - 1973 enrollments increased in kindergarten, primary, secondary, and postsecondary schools. The university system was made tuition free leading to an 89% rise in the number of students. The illiteracy rate was decreased from 12% in 1970 to 10% in 1972. The school enrollment rate of children 6 -14 increased from 91% to 99%. Social security payments were increased. Pensions were increased at 2 -4 times the inflation rate. The wage and salary adjustment program which had been introduced in the 1940's to cope with the chronic inflation was adjusted to raise salaries. The salaries of the armed forces were increased. Taxes were cut. Purchasing power of the average citizen initially rose 28% between October 1970 and July 1971.

Inflation fell from 36% in 1970 to 22% in 1971 while average real wages rose 22% in 1971. The short term effects of Minister of Economic Affairs Pedro Vuskovic's monetary expansion were positive with a 12% growth in industrial growth and 8.6% rise in GDP in 1971. Unfortunately, the piper had to be paid and by 1972 the inflation rate from this government spending was 140%. Inflation accelerated in 1972 with a basket of consumer goods rising by 120% in the month of August alone. Real GDP contracted in 1972 and 1973 at a rate of - 5.6% per year . The combination of inflation and government price fixing led to empty shelves at the grocery stores. Allende then announced he would default on debts owed foreign governments and international creditors.

In the period 1970-1972 exports fell 24 % and imports rose 26 % with imports of food rising 149%. Agricultural production dropped with land reform so Chile which was already dependent on food imports became more dependent. Chile's main export was copper, and unfortunately the world market price for copper fell from 66 dollars per ton to 49 dollars per ton (26 % decrease very similar to the drop in exports). Copper production declined following nationalization.

In May 1973 the Supreme Court of Chile unanimously denounced the Allende's disruption of the rule of law by its refusal to permit police execution of judicial decisions contrary to Allende's policies.

On August 22 1973 the members of the Chilean Congress voted 81 to 47 in favor of a resolution " to put an immediate end" to "the breaches of the Constitution."

The breaches Allende was charged with were:

1. Ruling by decree, circumventing the normal legislative system.
2. Refusing to enforce judicial decisions against his allies; not carrying out sentences and judicial resolutions that opposed the objectives of his administration.
3. Ignoring the decrees of the independent General Comptroller's Office.
4. Sundry media offenses; taking control of the National Television Network and applying economic pressure on media that were not unconditional supporters of the government.
5. Allowing its Socialists supporters to assemble with arms, and preventing the same by its right wing opponents.
6. Supporting more than 1500 illegal takeovers of farms.
7. Illegal repression of the El Teniente miner's strike.
8. Illegally limiting emigration.

The resolution condemned the creation and development of government protected armed groups. It also called attention to his "notorious attempts to use the armed and police forces for partisan ends, destroy their institutional hierarchy, and politically infiltrate their ranks."

On September 11,1973 General Augusto Pinochet staged a coup. During the coup, Allende gave a farewell speech on live radio. "Workers of my country, I have faith in Chile and its destiny. Other men will overcome this dark and bitter moment when treason seeks to prevail. Keep in mind that, much sooner than later, the great avenues will again be opened through which will pass free men to construct a better society. Long live Chile! Long live the people! Long live the workers!" Allende was killed during the coup, shot once with a small caliber fire arm and then reshot with an AK-47 to make it look like suicide.

Notes on Allende's brief time in power. Like many leftist he concentrated on the redistribution of wealth rather than the creation of it. He inherited a country with an ongoing inflation problem which is a sign the central government was already spending too much when he took over. Inflation was dropping during his first year in office which was probably a legacy effect from the previous administration although it was still in the double digits. He spent a lot of money on laudable goals such as education, maternal and childhood nutrition. However, he didn't have the money to accomplish all his ambitious plans at once and this led to a ruinous inflation. His abuse of the the capitalist class of people and his Marxist framing of the issues as matters of class struggle rather than National improvement did not attract a lot of the talented people he needed to persuade to help him.

Inflation fell from 34.1% to 22.1 % his first year in office with industrial output growing 12% and GDP growing 8.6%. After that exports fell (largely due to the drop in the price of copper) and imports increased 26% with food imports increasing 149%. This terrible balance of trade contributed to inflation rising to 140% in 1972 while real growth contracted to -1.2%. From December 1972 until December 1973 inflation was 508%, a catastrophic hyperinflation, meanwhile the growth in GDP was - 4.2%.

Nationalizations in the copper industry led to a drop in copper production, expropriations in agriculture led to a drop in food production exacerbating the inflation problems already baked into the cake.

If you are going to misrule this badly, you need to have the military and police on your side. They followed the Constitution while he did but when he destroyed the Constitutional legitimacy of his regime as above at the same time crashing the economy it was a set up for a coup.

Pinochet

Friedman

Policy then veered from a socialist plan to a neoliberal plan under General Pinochet. In 1973-1974 250 nationalized companies were given back to their former owners. In 1975 Chile began to implement plans which reflected the thinking of the economists from the University of Chicago (Milton Friedman) with the Chicago trained Sergio de Castro becoming minister of the economy. The Chicago Boys advocated free market economics with fiscal conservatism. They engineered a sharp recession to stop inflation (shock therapy). Businesses and lands nationalized under Allende were re-privatized (except for the copper industry which was used to fund the military government). Price controls were abolished and import tariffs reduced, capital flows were deregulated. The central bank raised interest rates from 49.9% to 178%.

The business community which had initially been supportive of these actions became disenchanted as manufacturing dropped by 26% in 1975. Real interest rates at 38%, hasty import liberalizations, and an artificially high currency contributed to a high rate of business failure.

The economy expanded from 1977 to 1980 with high growth rates averaging between 5 and 8 % a year. In 1982 the Latin American debt crisis hit. The GDP declined 14% in Chile, more than any other country. Dollarization was used to fight inflation. This led to a high current account deficit. Sergio de Castro rejected a competitive devaluation of the Peso in 1982 arguing that only the strongest and fittest should survive. Eventually Chile was forced to devalue and raise interest rates. There was a huge amount of private foreign debt. Foreign banks (Chase, Bankers Trust, etc) began to apply pressure to nationalize the foreign debt. <u>At first Finance Minister de Castro told them no - Chile was not going to assume responsibility for private debts. The banks cut off Chile's foreign trade credit lines causing oil tankers headed for Chile to turn around and go home.</u>[6] De Castro resigned in April 1982 and his successors had to socialize the two biggest Chilean banks in 1982 and seven more in 1983. The public expenditure quota rose above 34% - higher than Allende had ever achieved. (i.e. At this point Pinochet's neoliberal regime was forced to socialize more of the Chilean economy than Allende's avowedly socialist regime. Don't laugh too much, our national debt divided by our national wealth of 18 trillion / 54 trillion is 33%). This was called ,"the Chicago Road to Socialism". In January 1983 unemployment was 30%.

Later in the 1980's many of these firms were re-privatized with foreign financial institutions / banks and rich Chilean's getting great deals while the mass of the people did not reap very much.

Notes on the Chicago Road to Socialism.

Free trade tends to make countries have a less diversified economy which makes them more vulnerable to global financial storms. Having a more globally interdependent economy makes them more vulnerable to financial intimidation. With a less free trading economy Sergio de Castro could have told the banks that it was a private transaction and not the government's responsibility with greater impunity (Andrew Jackson would not have caved). Also the hot money that circulates would be less mobile and more committed in a less free trade economy. What we see is a pattern not just in Chile, but in the US, Ireland, Mexico that the government bailouts benefit not those in the greatest need, but those with the best government lobbyist, so the Darwinistic ethos espoused by free traders, even when they believe it in their hearts (even finance ministers can have hearts), is really just for the little guy and not the rich and powerful.

Free trade makes it difficult to control the internal milieu of a country. This led directly to the tragicomedy of Pinochet's Chile neoliberal dream economy being even more statist than Allende's bumbling socialist experiment. There is a ratcheting effect of these crises if they wipe out the small business but leave the larger entities intact of the large getting larger and the small entities going away. This form of Economic Darwinism is more difficult to justify because it depends on government connections for its longevity rather than serving a useful social function better and more economically than the competition.

We can see in this sad parable the two forces that have been tormenting average families in America, the nutty left and the international capitalist right failing to achieve a prosperous just society. One of the principal impediments to that achievement is failure to regulate trade flows and develop a diversified local economy that gives the opportunity to the people to work to solve their own problems. Without boundaries there is a loss of accountability, a loss of responsibility, and a loss of effectiveness.

This brings us to our next point.
Who wins with Free Trade?

The international capitalist achieves several things with Free Trade:

1. The ability to practice Plantation Capitalism. With access to all the world's misery, the capitalist gets the ability to price workers based on wherever they are most oppressed. He can source product from these miserable locations or with immigration bring these desperate people to where they can be used to drive down the wage scale at will. He can then sell his product where demand will give him a good profit. The oppressed workers are not his market.
2. The ability to avoid taxes especially on foreign sourced product. This is even more true because these desperate locations will likely give him favorable terms as long as the business he founds can be moved at will.
3. The ability to stash his wealth offshore where it is safe from the governments of the world.
4. The ability to have the family fortune independent of the fate of any one nation. In fact, in Latin America, we see that much of the wealth of the elites is offshore (Miami,

Switzerland, etc.). This allows them to buy assets in their country when times are desperate and sell when stability returns. Most privatizations are not like Abraham Lincoln's Homestead Act. The assets flow to people who are connected to money and away from the citizenry.
5. When the economic entities become powerful relative to the state, they can force the state to bail them out as in the savings and loan debacle, the bailouts associated with the housing crisis, Pinochet being forced to nationalize the private debts, etc.
6. When the business interests are powerful relative to the state, they can corrupt the state into doing their will (above and beyond the bailouts above).
7. The ability to avoid environmental laws by seeking locations to manufacture that do not protect the environment.
8. The ability to avoid worker safety laws by locating the jobs where regulation enforcement is lax.

The international left achieves several things with Free Trade:
1. The ability to empathize with the oppressed everywhere.
2. The ability to dream of working men of the world uniting. (Marx and Engels)
3. The ability to organize transnationally. (One suspects that the capitalists will out maneuver them. Further, one suspects that transnational entities will tend to be corrupted to serve the need of the capitalists whose money will talk. The disparate citizens of the world will be divided by language, race, religion, and wealth; they will have a difficult time uniting on a common message unless little green men from Mars show up.)
4. The ability to daydream of an international tax on capital. (Mr. Piketty. Good luck with that one.)
5. The ability to say that they are not national socialists

until they take over a country. Then they invariably are running a nation and they are socialists. Note Allende's final words: "Long live Chile! Long live the people! Long live the workers!"

The above shows that the advantages that accrue to the Capitalist are of a concrete palpable nature which can be translated easily into cold hard cash where as the advantages to the Left are of a romantic whimsical nature unlikely to produce a better world for the workers because they won't be implemented under any sort of normal conditions and when implemented will likely lead to disasters and unintended consequences.

Let's invert the image and look at the losses associated with Free Trade:

1. Loss of salary. Decreased salaries in developed countries.
2. Loss of wealth. (Increased indebtedness.) In 1832 when Henry Clay gave his American System speech, Andrew Jackson was getting ready to pay off the national debt. That was after two wars with the most powerful country on the planet, Great Britain, and the Louisiana Purchase. Currently we are in debt 18.2 trillion dollars after fighting Afghanistan and Iraq?!
Private debt has also increased in the US. We are not alone; many other nations are bound in debt as well.
3. Loss of tax base.
4. Loss of industrial prowess.
5. Loss of babies. (Decreased birth rate.) Adam Smith says this is the best judge of living standards of the workers.
6. Loss of national security.
7. Loss of the war on drugs.
8. Corruption of the state to bailout huge boondoggles.

9. Loss of freedom as we create a Department of Homeland Security to form a police state to promote security in a country that would be perfectly secure if it simply enforced its borders.
10. Loss of accountability. The general sense of failure means that government is no longer held to a standard of performance.
11. Loss of middle class expectations of prosperity through work. Increasing class tensions.

12. With the increasing class tension, democracy works less well with a hardening of positions. It becomes more difficult to find a consensus.

Digression on Marx, Aristotle, and Nationhood.

"Merchants have no country."

-Thomas Jefferson

"Workingmen have no country."

-Karl Marx

"Man is by nature a social animal; an individual who is unsocial naturally and not accidentally is either beneath our notice or more than human. Society is something that precedes the individual. Anyone who either cannot lead the common life or is so self sufficient as not to need to, and therefore does not partake of society, is either a beast or a god."

- Aristotle

There are two simultaneous realities. People live in countries and are social. People tend their own self interest. Adam Smith emphasized the reality that people tend their own self interest and this instinct is so powerful and fundamental to human behavior that it strongly predicts what people will do. He emphasized that while being primarily motivated by "what's in it for me", the cooperative arrangements of society would channel much of this behavior for the common good (the invisible hand at work). Marx absorbed much of this at a foundational level and chose as his protagonist the bourgeois, the capitalist class that he saw disrupting ancient Europe and remaking Europe in their image. This was his Hegelian thesis. He then chose the proletariat as his antithesis and he framed all of history as class struggle.

He then labored mightily to put everyone into this paradigm which is in a sense an extension of Adam Smith's free trade paradigm. "The lower strata of the middle class- the small tradespeople, shopkeepers, and retired tradespeople generally, the handicraftsmen and peasants- all these sink gradually into the proletariat." This may have some physical reality, but really he is just putting everyone who is not a major capitalist into his proletariat box so it will fit his Hegelian paradigm. Since the merchants do not have a country and are practicing globalized free trade, Marx's antithesis, the proletariat, must also be an international proletariat. Leftist thinking has been muddled ever since.

Hegelian thinking when projecting into the future is limited by the thesis, because many of the features of the antitheses will be determined by the thesis. Thus a flawed view of the thesis will make it almost impossible to get back to reality. One of the ancient problems of math was how to construct a trisection of an angle with a compass and straightedge. Finally in 1837 Pierre Wantzel, a French mathematician, showed that the problem corresponds to the solution of a cubic equation and was not in general solvable. Much as you can't trisect an angle using only a straight edge and a compass because your tools are insufficient, you can't predict the future with a Hegelian model when your paradigm is that all of history is class struggle and your only two protagonists are international capitalists and international proletariat. The extension field of your thought won't match the field of reality.

Workmen do have a country. It's where they live. Plantation capitalists do attempt with some success to commoditize the workers, but that is far from the whole story.

The world is in general divided up into countries. This is where people actually live. It is where the actual markets are that people sell things; it's where the actual factories are where they make things; it's where the actual fields are that they grow things; it's where the actual mountains are that they mine things.

To go further, even the merchants have a country. It is true that as pure economic entities they may be a pure internationalist, but as the story of the Vestey's shows, they want to live in their own culture surrounded by the people they love and who love them just like everybody else. Unlike everybody else they are less economically committed to any one country and have greater ability to hide their money from the tax man.

Within each country laws will be made to regulate the interactions of the population, and governments will be formed to make and enforce the laws. Countries will be different based on language, power structures, education, religion, geography, challenges, and opportunities. The laws that a country enacts and enforces can have a profound impact on the quality of life of her citizens. Free trade advocates would have you believe that laws that regulate trade only get in the way of progress. If the progress you seek is to commoditize the workers, to relieve the capitalist from the drudgery of paying taxes, to degrade the environment, and to have the state do the will of the capitalists, then to have the government slink away into obscurity is the answer. But if you believe in a collective future where people are valued and the nation makes gifts to the global tapestry in thought, manufacture, and art you will not so quickly renounce the nation state because this at present is the only entity with the strength to protect the citizenry from those corporate forces that wish to commoditize and degrade them.

This is where the American System, and indeed all trust based capitalisms, leaves the Free Trade advocates and their antithesis, the Marxist International Left, behind. The American System is based on regulation of trade flows to promote a general national prosperity encompassing the capitalist and the worker, but also the small shopkeeper, the self employed, the artist, and your local orthodontist. We can expect, and have historical reasons to expect, that the general prosperity will make the worker more valued by the capitalist, and the capitalist richer because he will have a richer market to sell into. There will be negotiations over wages, for sure, but not an epic class struggle. It won't be a zero sum game; everyone who wants to win can. The American System will build a stronger community.

At a deeper more spiritual level, continuity of the nation is important because it serves a framework for Aristotle's common life to have meaning. Within our language, laws, customs, beliefs, and religions our actions have meaning, our sacrifices are understood, the legacy of what we loved preserved. If we are so weak as to allow ourselves to be commoditized, all of this is in jeopardy. Much of our struggle with militant Islam can be understood in terms of economics and power, but there is a definite spiritual side to the conflict, where these violent young men want to leave a legacy in the world. The general public of Europe has great distrust about giving up their nationhood to a bunch of faceless bureaucrats who want to commoditize them in the welfare state for much the same reason. This common life is closely connected to manhood, the freedom and the power to take responsibility for one's society and life. It should not be lightly set aside for a bunch of Davos elites. It should not be set aside at all.

*

1. Phillip Knightley, "The Vestey Affair",(London:Macdonald Fututura Publishers), p16.
2. Ibid, p 28.
3. Ibid, p 34- 35.
4. Ibid, p 35 -37.
5. James S. Henry, "The Blood Bankers", (Four Walls Eight Windows 2003), p 26 - 27.
6. Alan Taylor, "American Colonies,The Settling of North America,(Penguin Books 2001), p 221.
7. James S. Henry, "The Blood Bankers", (Four Walls Eight Windows 2003), p 272 -273.

Theodore
Schwann

Matthias
Schleiden

Rudolph
Virchow

Schwann and Schleiden are given credit for developing cell theory:

1. All living organisms are cells.
2. The cell is the most basic unit of life.

Virchow added that:

3. All cells arise from other cells.

Much as recognizing that animals are cellular organisms is vital to the study of biology, recognizing that people are social animals organized into nation states, which like cells have boundaries, is fundamental to any scientific study of economics.

Courses of Action

"Thou shalt bring them in,
and plant them in the mountain of thine inheritance,
in the place, O Lord,
which thou hast made for thee to dwell in,
in the Sanctuary, O Lord,
which thy hands have established."

-Exodus 15:17

"The condition upon which God hath given liberty to man is eternal vigilance; which condition if he break, servitude is at once the consequence of his crime and the punishment of his guilt."

To Americans, America is the promised land. It is where with hard work dreams become reality. It is where with Divine Providence the bare bones of ideas become clothed in flesh. This began with our Pilgrim forefathers setting out on a journey to found a colony where they might worship God as they chose and raise their children to fear the Lord. It is where 150 years later our Founding Fathers declared themselves free and conceived a republic dedicated to the principal that all men are created equal and endowed by their Creator with certain inalienable rights. The Constitution is a covenant of hope, that a free people taking responsibility for their actions, can live fruitful lives and bring the blessings of liberty on themselves and their posterity.

We have had trials. There have been trials of war where

we have been tested at Valley Forge, at Gettysburg, at the Battle of the Bulge, and many other hard fields. More hard fields lie ahead. We have had economic trials. We have had a long struggle for human dignity and freedom to redeem the promise for all Americans best epitomized by peaceful yet forceful ministry of Dr. Martin Luther King, Jr. We are currently at a similar moment of decision.

Our Nationhood is currently under assault by people and institutions that have benefited the most from a strong free America. These people have benefited from a doctrine of Free Trade by sourcing product in foreign lands where people are oppressed or importing oppressed people here with the malignant intention of disrupting the salary scale to their benefit. In this work I have designated such people and institutions as Plantation Capitalists because at root their business plan is little changed from a Barbados sugar plantation - they make their margin oppressing labor and sell their product somewhere else because the people they oppress can't buy it. This has been a constant struggle throughout our history.

What is new is the rhetoric of globalization - that somehow we are evil or backward for wanting our borders enforced. Many of these people are so politically correct they won't say they are nationalistic, but it's OK to be patriotic. What these people don't say is that the number one asset of most Americans is that they are Americans in America. When this is diluted, you are diluting the principle resource most American's have. Billionaires Buffet, Adelson, and Gates might have a different feeling about immigration if the argument that he is a good guy, so distribute your primary asset to the foreigners extended from the little guy's citizenship to the rich man's stock portfolio. What is also new and quite related to globalization is our trade deficit, large private debt, and large public debt. With the trade deficit we would go into deflationary collapse without massive deficit public spending. I have used the imagery of lamprey capitalism to illuminate this parasitic life draining process.

I have used the imagery of the cell and the cell membrane to indicate that just because we want our boundary enforced does not mean we do not want to cooperate with other Nations and peoples any more than one cell of your body doesn't want to work with the other cells of your body. We just want our interactions regulated in a way that preserves the economic vitality of our country, and we want the other people of the world to also have healthy happy communities of their own. Furthermore, if the cells of your body at a microscopic level can regulate what is on one side of a cell membrane and what is on the other, the notion that we as a nation can't control our borders is nonsense. The Plantation Capitalists, drug lords, and terrorists just don't want us to control our borders, but we can. We can maintain an internal milieu in this country where a people can find meaningful work, found and raise a family, and live in peace enjoying this great country.

Who is globalization good for? It is good for the rich and the powerful who can take the options of the world and practice Plantation Capitalism destroying the wage scale and financial strength of the nations that host them. It helps the powerful and rich avoid taxes. Meanwhile, throughout the developed world the birth rate has collapsed, which is a sign of sadness and oppression. Can the individual middle class worker benefit from Globalization? In aggregate, so far, not so much.

The best protection that a worker can have against these forces is to reside in a strong nation state that looks after his interest. China is the most obvious example. Japan did well for a long time but currently has significant problems. Russia is an interesting example. After the collapse of the Soviet Union, Russia was looted like a deer carcass being eaten by vultures- the tender mercies of unfettered globalization. Putin put an end to this, reestablishing a strong central government. He is popular in Russia because even a borderline kleptocratic strong central government is better for the average Russian than a free market looting of one's country.

What practically is to be done?

1) We need to return to the American System of Alexander Hamilton, Henry Clay, and Abraham Lincoln. We need to reestablish our border and aim for self sufficiency. The first most obvious step is to switch to a consumption tax that falls on the Chinese and the Plantation Capitalists - replace the Social Security Tax, Medicare Tax with a 40% tariff. With a wage differential on the order of 5 to one between Mexico, China, and India vs. the US even this may be insufficient but it would be a start. We could then follow the Shewhart / Deming cycle of Plan - Do - Check - Act until our trade deficit is stabilized. As foreign trade drops off, it will be easier to police our borders with respect to drugs, human trafficking, and malicious spy operations.

2) We need to enforce our borders with respect to immigration. The diversity talk is distracting propaganda used to obscure the purpose of the Plantation Capitalists to destroy our wage scale for their benefit. Unfortunately, you cannot enforce a rule and show mercy at the same time. All parents know this; it leads to chaos. That said, the workers who are here are not the true criminals in this situation and enforcement needs to be as humane as possible respecting the property that these people have acquired in their sojourn in America. In a sense this is like the parent putting the oxygen on in an airplane emergency before assisting the child. If we are going to enforce the Monroe doctrine, we have a responsibility not to let the people of Latin America (especially Mexico) be exploited so they don't end up being colonized by foreign countries. With the resources we have in

the Western Hemisphere everyone should be rich from Baffin Island to Tierra del Fuego. This can and should be done, but first we need to restore our economy and our wage scale.

3) We need debt relief for the middle class. A forgiveness of student loans would be a start. The paper chains of debt which the Plantation Capitalists have made for the American Middle Class must be destroyed so our children can live free in the promised land.

I will finish with a quote from William Bradford on the decision to brave the risks of voyage, exploration, and colony foundation with respect to the Pilgrims leaving Holland and coming to America.

> "It was answered that all great and honorable actions are accompanied with great difficulties and must be both enterprised and overcome with answerable courages. It was granted the dangers were great, but not desperate. The difficulties were many, but not invincible. For though there were many of them likely, yet they were not certain. It might be sundry of the things feared might never befall; others by provident care and the use of good means might in great measure be prevented; and all of them, through the help of God, by fortitude and patience, might either be borne or overcome. True it was that such attempts were not to be made and undertaken without good ground and reason, not rashly or lightly as many have done for curiosity or hope of gain, etc. But their condition was not ordinary, their ends were good and honorable, their calling lawful and urgent; and therefore they might expect the blessing of God in their proceeding. Yea, though they should lose their lives in this action, yet might they have comfort in the same and their endeavors would be honorable. They lived here but as

men in exile and in a poor condition, and as great miseries might possibly befall them in this place; for the twelve years of truce were now out and there was nothing but the beating of drums and preparing for war, the events whereof are always uncertain. The Spaniard might prove as cruel as the savages of America, and the famine and pestilence as sore here as there, and their liberty less to look out for remedy.

After many other particular things answered and alleged on both sides, it was fully concluded by the major part to put this design in execution and to prosecute it by the best means they could."